CLOUD DATABASE SECURITY: INTEGRATING DEEP LEARNING AND MACHINE LEARNING FOR THREAT DETECTION AND PREVENTION

Rajendra Prasad Sola

Nihar Malali

Praveen Madugula

Made with ❤ on the Notion Press Platform
www.notionpress.com

PREFACE

From the exponential growth of Cloud Computing, business as well as individual now defines how they can manage and secure data. With organizations moving their workloads to the cloud, it becomes undeniable that strong security measures are needed. This book, Cloud Database Security: Integrating DL and ML for Threat Detection and Prevention discusses how the landscape of cloud database security is evolving and how powerful technologies such as Deep Learning (DL) and Machine Learning (ML) can be integrated in order to prevent threats.

It is the product of years of research, practical insight and technological exploration. Taking it chapter by chapter, each tries to demystify complex problems, explaining cloud security challenges and their solutions in a clear and structured way. This book aims to act as a comprehensive guide for students, professionals and researchers in the area of cloud computing and cybersecurity by combining foundational knowledge with cutting edge applications.

Hope this book would not only teach, but also encourage readers to come up with and actively participate in the ongoing field of cybersecurity.

DEDICATION

Rajendra Prasad Sola

This book is dedicated to a guiding light, a source of inspiration, and unwavering support. Your wisdom, kindness, and strength have left an indelible mark on this journey, and for that, I am forever grateful.

Nihar Malali

This book is dedicated to

the three goddesses in my life:

my mother, Geeta,

my wife, Sushma,

and my daughter, Araina

Praveen Madugula

This book is dedicated to a true source of encouragement and motivation. Your belief, guidance, and steadfast support have been instrumental in shaping this journey, and I am deeply thankful for your presence along the way.

ACKNOWLEDGEMENT

Writing this book has been part discovery and part collaboration. We want to give a very big thanks to so many of people that We have done this with and each of them has been a huge part of the reason that this is even a possibility today.

We want to express my deepest gratitude to my mentors and colleagues for their enormously valuable input and supportive feedback. This book represents the fruits of their expertise, which have driven both its content and its structure.

Many thanks to my family and friends who had always been my source of encouragement and patience as we spent many hours of research and writing.

We want to thank the publisher and the editor who handled this manuscript with professionalism and good sense of duties to render it a nice work.

We conclude by thanking the readers whose interest in learning has driven work like this. We wish this book will satisfy your expectations and proves to you as the useful resource in your way.

Thank you.

CONTENTS

3. Threat Detection Using Machine Learning and Deep Learning   87

4. Preventing Threats Using Ai-Driven Security Mechanisms   **118**

5. Recent Developments in Cloud Database Security   **161**

Chapter 01

INTRODUCTION TO CLOUD DATABASE SECURITY

1.1 Chapter Overview

The first chapter is "Introduction to Cloud Database Security," which provides an extensive background on Cloud computing, database systems and, more importantly, the security risks that arise with their combination. This chapter brings the reader closer to apprehending the aspects of the risk of Cloud database and the opportunities towards its protection using modern technologies such as Deep Learning (DL) and Machine Learning (ML).

In the first place, the authors permit himself to deliver a precise definition of Cloud computing and its importance in the contemporary IT landscape. It expands on the prevalent idea of providing services like databases on-demand through Cloud and the ability these present to offer businesses affordable services without the need for the buildings that were once required to host the services. The chapter also presents some of the Cloud database systems like Relational, NoSQL and Cloud native database offer different strengths and weaknesses namely on the security aspect.

Subsequently, the forthcoming chapter of the work delves into the fundamental security concerns that impact Cloud databases, with focal points on the shared responsibility model, data privacy and protection, API weaknesses, dynamic misconfigurations, and Cloud migration risks. It also looks at how these threats to Cloud environments can open up security vulnerabilities and make it easy for cyber criminals to attack.

This then brings us to the next chapter, which takes a closer look at the protection aspect of threat detection in Cloud security, this elaborates on how an organization can adopt preventive security measures to ensure that threats are detected, fought off and neutralized in the best way possible. This section describes the practices of old Generation security models being transformed to fit within contemporary Cloud needs.

In addition, the requirements of reliable data protection measures are described, with examination of the priorities such as availability, confidentiality, and integrity of data. The last section of the chapter gives special emphasis on how AI and ML are becoming central in security protection of Cloud networks with regards to threat assessments, prevention, and handling of incidents through more reliable, timely and autonomous schemes. This chapter serves as the introduction to the necessity of actualizing more sophisticated artificial intelligent solutions as the only means for protecting Cloud databases from new and emerging threats.

Deep Learning (DL) and Machine Learning (ML) have emerged as transformative tools in enhancing the security of Cloud databases, offering sophisticated mechanisms for detecting and preventing threats. As key subsets of Artificial Intelligence (AI), ML focuses on recognizing patterns and making decisions based on data, while DL, a more advanced form of ML, employs neural networks to analyze complex data structures. These technologies complement each other, creating a robust framework for addressing the dynamic challenges posed by modern cyber threats.

In Cloud database security, ML algorithms analyze extensive datasets to detect anomalies that may signal potential security breaches. By training models on historical security logs and attack patterns, ML systems can identify unusual user behavior, unauthorized access attempts, or irregular query patterns. Supervised ML techniques, such as decision trees, classify activities into normal and suspicious categories, while unsupervised methods, like clustering algorithms, excel at identifying novel threats. This adaptability ensures that ML evolves alongside emerging threats, providing a continuous and dynamic defense.

DL adds an extra layer of sophistication, particularly in processing and interpreting unstructured or complex data such as system logs, API interactions, or traffic patterns. Using layered neural networks, DL models can uncover intricate relationships within data, allowing for the detection of advanced threats like zero-day attacks. Recurrent neural networks (RNNs) are particularly effective in analyzing sequential data, while other neural network architectures can identify patterns that traditional methods might miss. The continuous learning capability of DL ensures improved accuracy and reduced false positives over time.

Beyond threat detection, DL and ML play a pivotal role in prevention and mitigation. Predictive analytics powered by these technologies helps organizations anticipate vulnerabilities, enabling proactive measures. These models can automate incident responses, identify the nature of threats, and deploy countermeasures in real-time, minimizing response time and human error.

In ensuring data confidentiality, integrity, and availability, DL and ML have proven indispensable. By safeguarding sensitive information and fortifying systems against unauthorized access, these technologies enable a more secure and resilient Cloud database environment, addressing the evolving landscape of cybersecurity threats effectively.

1.2 Understanding Cloud Computing and Database Systems

There has been much discussion on the benefits and drawbacks of Cloud computing. It becomes crucial to have a conversation about database deployment on Cloud infrastructure. The phrase Cloud Database, or Cloud DB, refers to the marriage of Cloud technology with database. I would want to use this opportunity to examine the Cloud solutions and the data requirements of the organization in detail.

The word A Cloud database is a database system that is built on top of a Cloud platform and provides services via it. The platform-as-a-service concept essentially makes it simple to arrange apps that store, modify, and retrieve data from Cloud infrastructure. A common database service or solution, Cloud DB is set up on a Cloud platform by installing database software on top of it. Databases are immediately accessed over the web or through APIs offered by programs.

The use of Cloud platforms, infrastructures, and services has increased dramatically in recent years. When Cloud technology and databases are combined, there is a greater need for management research and development. There are concerns regarding Cloud database administration and security because the data is dispersed and fragmented online. Data must be extremely precise, integrated, and consistent in order to meet the fundamental requirements of any organization. Information should be accessible when needed. and synchronized with the information in your database on-premises. In contrast to traditional database systems, Cloud computing offers run-time scalability, elastic resource utilization, and optimum performance, making it the best choice for this purpose.

Among the numerous benefits that Cloud database, also known as database-as-a-service (DaaS), offers businesses are quick deployment technologies, lower system investment and maintenance costs, and—above all—the ability to adapt to changing business requirements. Data must be protected from both known and undiscovered risks by the organization. This is the most crucial element. Despite the widespread acceptance of Cloud computing, businesses are still reluctant to save their data on the Cloud. Even now, most organizations hide their servers when questioned about using Cloud platforms to deploy databases. Since data must be transported outside of firewalls and stored on Cloud servers, the security of business-critical data is a major problem for organizations(Relan, 2023).

Benefits they get from traditional database over Cloud services systems like:

- Parallel and Distributed Query Processing (again, clustering databases over the Cloud is a concern)

- Security and Privacy

- Storage Technologies and Architectures (since storage in the Cloud is completely concealed)

- System States and Analytics (Meta Data about system performance and the correctness of system parameter values that may be used to establish performance benchmarks because servers are virtual)

- Comparing and taking into account the dedicated database server's high availability when discussing Cloud database.

- Management of Workload and Resources Managing database burden is an issue or doubt for organisations as Cloud servers are already operational and functioning as resource management of the base nodes/hardware.

- Data Algorithms and Structures for Reliable Stores.

- Load-balancing, networks, and caching.

Cloud database services are offered by several suppliers, but administration of the aforementioned truly requires study and development. Without a question, Cloud computing is the finest technology available today, but in order to make Cloud database a new standard and more widely used, Cloud suppliers need to talk to database vendors.

What is Cloud computing?

The on-demand, pay-as-you-go online distribution of IT resources is known as Cloud computing. You may use a Cloud provider like Amazon Web Services (AWS) to obtain technological services like databases, storage, and processing power on an as-needed basis rather than purchasing, owning, and maintaining physical data centers and servers.

Both big and small IT firms supply their IT infrastructure using conventional techniques. This implies that a server room is a fundamental requirement for any IT organisation.

A database server, mail server, networking, firewalls, routers, modems, switches, QPS (Query Per Second, or how many queries or load the server will manage), a customizable system, fast internet, and maintenance engineers should all be present in one server room. It will cost a lot of money to set up such IT infrastructure. Cloud computing was created to address all of these issues and lower the cost of IT infrastructure.

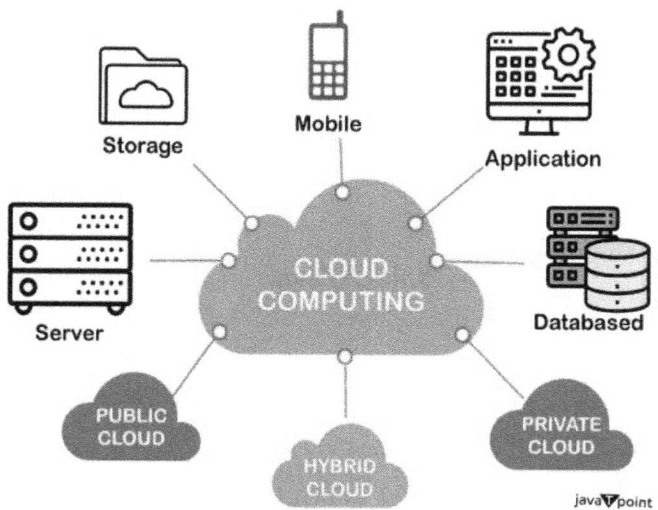

Source: - *(javatpoint, 2023)*

Characteristics of Cloud Computing

The following lists the features of Cloud computing:

1. **Agility**: A distributed computing environment is where the Cloud operates. It operates quickly and distributes resources among users.

2. **High availability and reliability**: Server availability is strong and more dependable due to the low likelihood of infrastructure failure.

3. **High Scalability**: Cloud computing provides large-scale "on-demand" resource provisioning without the need for engineers during peak demands.

4. **Multi-Sharing**: By sharing infrastructure, Cloud computing enables several users and applications to operate more effectively and affordably.

5. **Device and Location Independence**: Users may access systems through a web browser thanks to Cloud computing, regardless of where they are or what device they are using—a PC, smartphone, etc. Because the infrastructure is off-site (usually supplied by a third party) and accessible online, users can join from any location.

6. **Maintenance**: Applications for Cloud computing are easier to maintain since they may be accessed from several locations and don't need to be installed on each user's machine. Thus, it also lowers the cost.

7. **Low Cost**: Utilising Cloud computing will save money since it eliminates the need for IT companies to build up their own infrastructure and pay for resources based on consumption.

8. **Services in the pay-per-use mode**: Users are given access to Application Programming Interfaces (APIs) so they may use them to access Cloud services and pay for such services based on their usage.

Types of Cloud

The following five Cloud types can be implemented based on the requirements of the company-

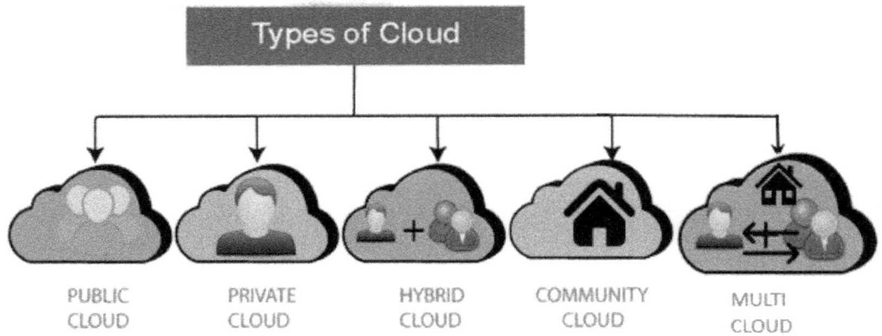

Source: - *(javatpoint, 2023)*

1.   **Public Cloud**

Using the pay-per-use model, public Clouds allow anybody to store and retrieve data over the Internet.

The Cloud Service Provider (CSP) is in charge of managing and running the computer resources in a public Cloud. The CSP maintains the auxiliary infrastructure and guarantees that the resources are scalable and available to consumers.

The public Cloud's open design allows anybody with an internet connection to access it, regardless of geography or business size. Users can run apps, save data, and utilize the many services offered by the CSP. Customers can be guaranteed they will only be billed for the resources they really use by implementing a pay-per-usage plan, which is a wise financial decision.

Example: Windows Azure Services Platform, Google App Engine, Microsoft, IBM Smart Cloud Enterprise, and Amazon Elastic Compute Cloud (EC2).

2. Private Cloud

Internal or corporate Clouds are other names for private Clouds. Organizations use it to construct and run their own data centers, either in-house or through a third party. Opensource technologies like Eucalyptus and Open stack can be used to deploy it.

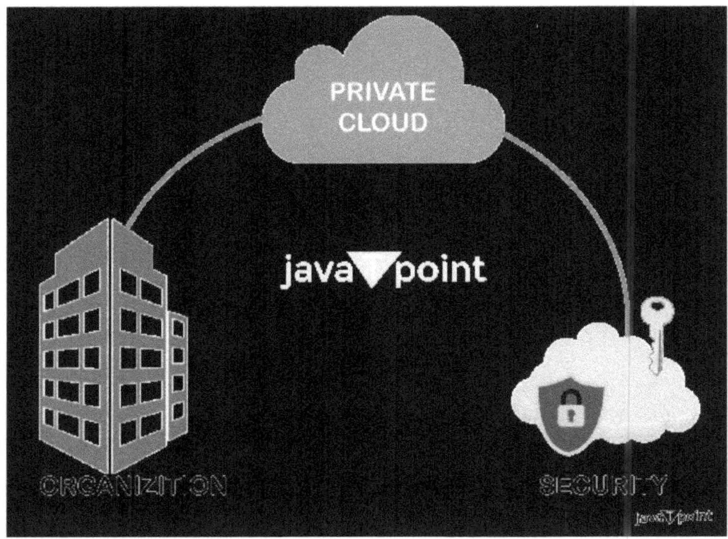

Examples: Oracle Cloud at Customer, OpenStack, Microsoft Azure Stack, VMware vSphere, and IBM Cloud Private.

3. Hybrid Cloud

A hybrid Cloud combines elements of both private and public Clouds, we can state:

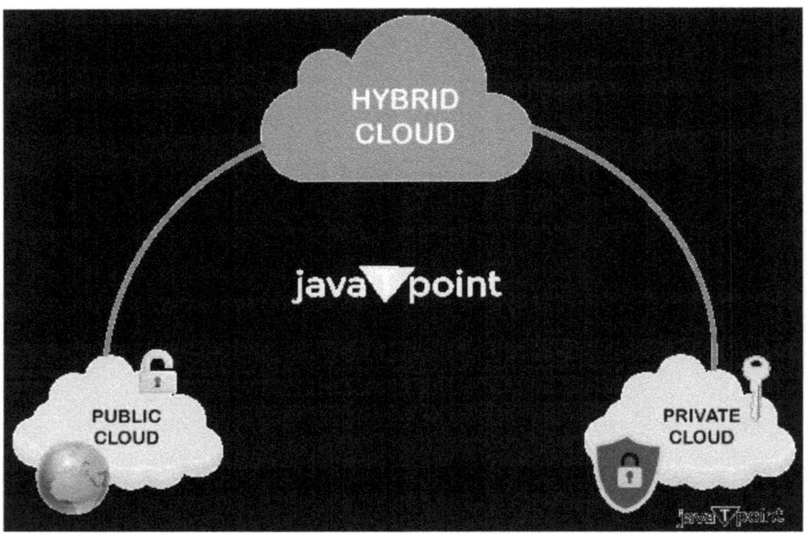

Hybrid Cloud = Public Cloud + Private Cloud

Because services on the public Cloud are accessible to everyone, while those on the private Cloud are restricted to the users of the organization, hybrid Cloud computing is only partially secure. With a hybrid Cloud configuration, businesses may take use of both private and public Cloud advantages to build a scalable and adaptable computing environment. Through the Internet, third-party providers' Cloud services can be accessed through the public Cloud section.

Example: Amazon Web Services, Office 365 (including One Drive and Microsoft Office on the Web), and Google Application Suite (including Gmail, Google Apps, and Google Drive).

4. Community Cloud

A collection of organizations can access systems and services through a community Cloud, which facilitates information sharing between the organization and a particular community. One or more community organizations, a third party, or a combination of them own, run, and maintain it.

The participating organizations, which may come from the same industry, government agency, or any other group, work together to create a shared Cloud infrastructure in a community Cloud setup. They may access community-relevant data, apps, and shared services thanks to this infrastructure.

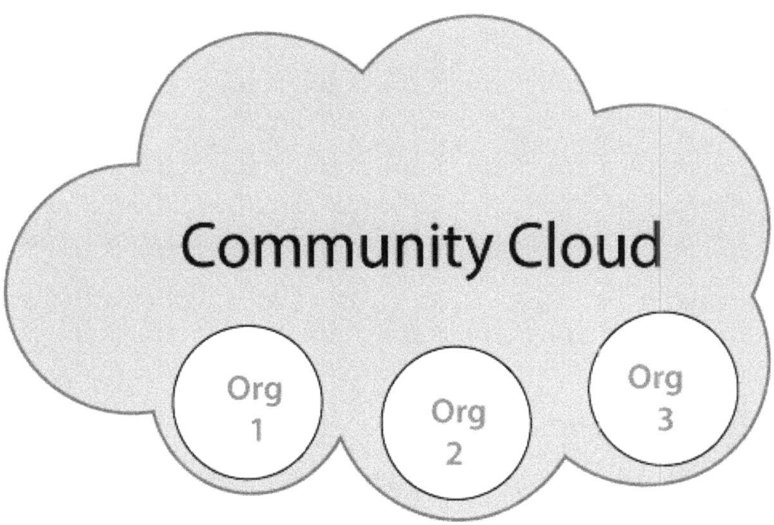

Example: Health Care community Cloud

5. Multi-Cloud

Businesses use many Cloud service providers or platforms to satisfy their computing demands as part of the multi-Cloud strategy. Workloads, apps, and statistics are dispersed over several Cloud environments, including public, private, and hybrid Clouds.

Implementing a multi-cloud strategy enables companies to choose and utilize the best Cloud services from many suppliers according to their unique needs. This reduces the danger of depending just on one vendor and gives them access to competitive pricing models by enabling them to capitalize on each provider's unique skills and services.

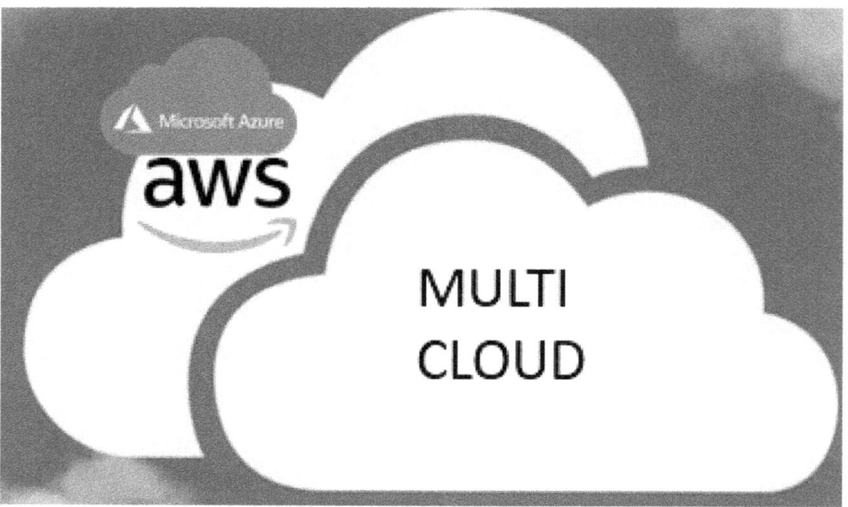

Examples: Microsoft Azure, Google Cloud Platform (GCP), and Amazon Web Services (AWS).

Database Defined

An organized collection of structured data, or information, usually kept electronically in a computer system, is called a database. Typically, a database management system (DBMS) controls a database. The term "database system," which is frequently abbreviated to "database," refers to the data, the DBMS, and the related applications.

To make processing and data querying more effective, data in the most popular database formats now in use is usually modelled in rows and columns in a sequence of tables. After that, it will be simple to access, manage, update, control, and organize the data. The majority of databases write and query data using structured query language (SQL).

DBMS can be classified into two main types:

1. Relational Database Management System (RDBMS)

2. Non-Relational Database Management System (NoSQL or Non-SQL)

Types of Databases

A basic explanation of the various database types is provided here.

1. Hierarchical Databases

This database tracks the evolution of data being categorized in ranks or levels, where data is categorized based on a common connection, much like any other hierarchy. Consequently, the commonality will assume a higher rank and two data entities will have a lower rank. Take a look at the diagram below:

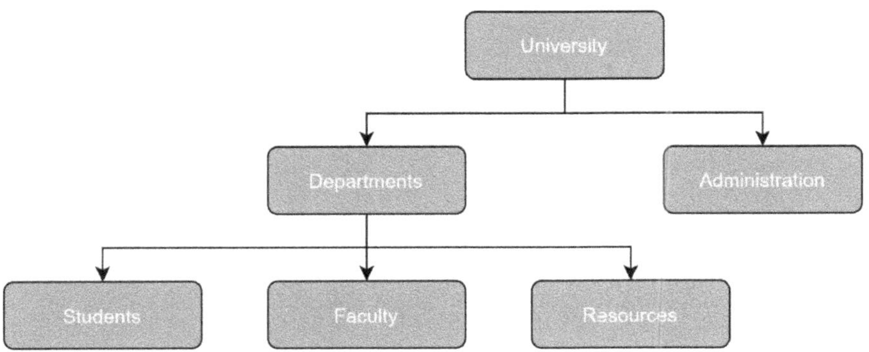

Hierarchical Database Example

Take note of how departments and administration are quite different from one another, although they are both part of a university. These components make up this structure.

Another viewpoint suggests arranging the data in a parent-child connection, which would resemble a tree as more data components are added. A field is used to link the child records to the parent record, allowing the parent record to have more than one child record. But the opposite isn't feasible.

It should be noted that hierarchical databases are difficult to scale because of their structure; adding data pieces necessitates a time-consuming database traversal.

2. Network Databases

Layman defines a network database as a hierarchical database that has undergone substantial alteration. The kid records have the option to be associated with several parent records. As a result, a network or net of database files linked to several threads may be seen. Note how the Student, Faculty, and Resources components are parent records for the Departments and Clubs.

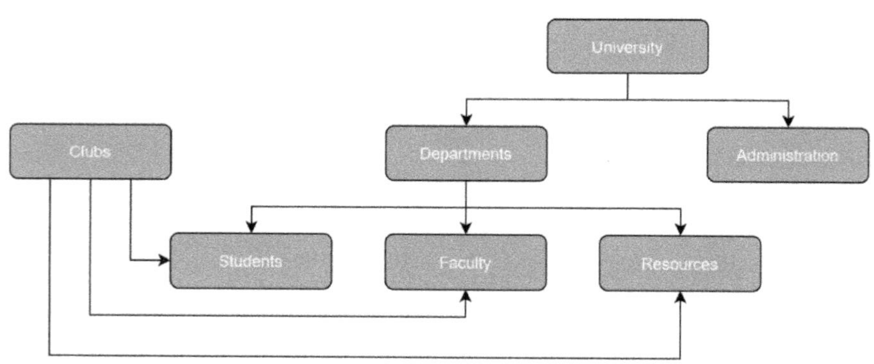

Network Database Example

Network databases are undoubtedly better at expressing two-way interactions in complicated frameworks. Additionally, using a more straightforward database management language is encouraged by conceptual simplicity.

The difficulty to change the structure because of its complexity and high degree of structural dependence is the drawback.

3. Object-Oriented Databases

This database schema is immediately relatable to those who are familiar with the Object-Oriented Programming Paradigm. It is possible to represent data contained in a database as an object that reacts as an instance of the database model. As a consequence, calling and referencing the object is simple. Consequently, the database's burden is significantly decreased.

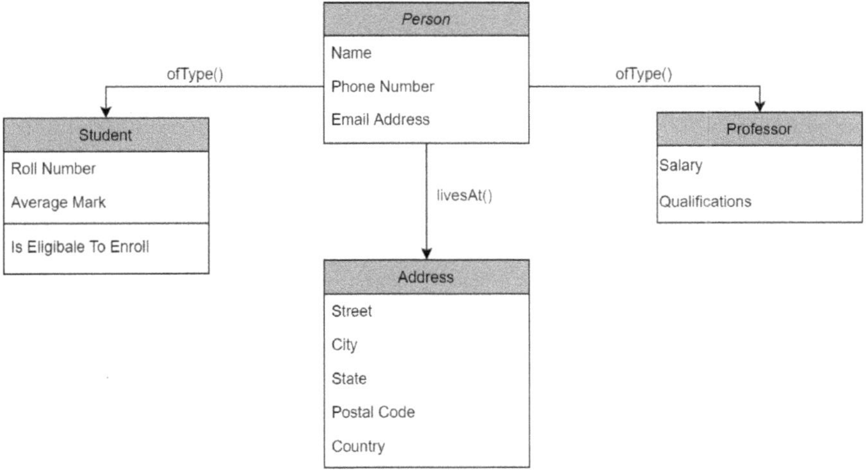

4. Object-Oriented Example

Several objects in the above chart are connected to one another via methods; the latest () method may be used to retrieve the address of the Person (represented by the Person Object). Additionally, the properties of these objects are found in the data elements that must be specified in the database.

The Berkeley DB software library is an example of such a paradigm, using the same conceptual foundation to provide fast and extremely effective answers to database queries from the embedded database.

5. Relational Databases

These databases, together with associated management systems, are thought to be the most developed of all databases and are at the forefront of the production line. Every item of information in this database is related to every other piece of information. This is because each record in the database represents a distinct identity for each data item.

Keep in mind that this model tabulates all data. As a result, a primary key connects each row of data in the database to every other row. In a same manner, a foreign key connects each table to every other table.

Refer the following graphic to see how two tables are connected using the idea of "Keys".

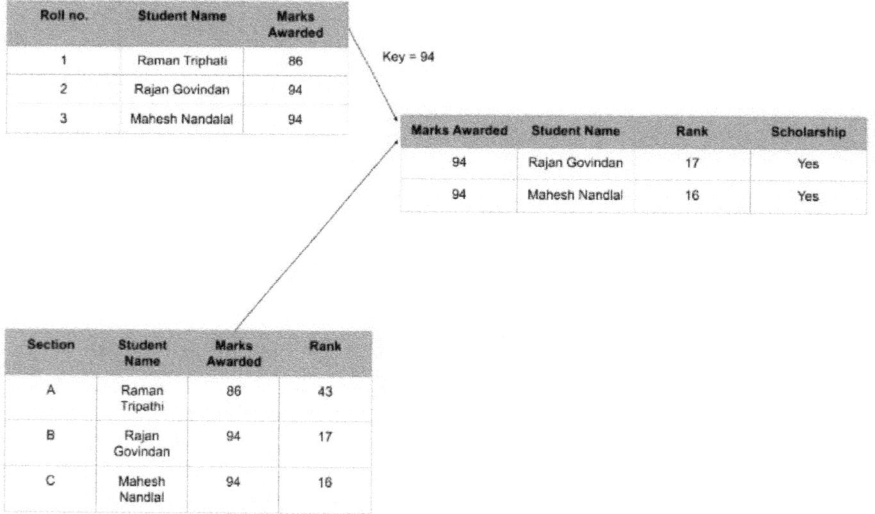

Relational Database Example

It has gained immense popularity as a result of the advent of tables for data organization. As a result, they are frequently incorporated into Web-Ap interfaces to act as perfect storage for user information. Because the language used to interface with the database is straightforward (in this example, SQL) and easy to understand, what makes it even more intriguing is how simple it is to learn.

It's also important to remember that, in contrast to hierarchical databases, scalability and data traversal are very simple tasks in relational databases.

6. Cloud Databases

There are several Cloud computing services available for retrieving data from databases (such as SaaS, PaaS, etc.), and Cloud databases are utilized when data needs a virtual environment for storage and execution across Cloud platforms.

There are some names of Cloud platforms are-

- Amazon Web Services (AWS)

- Google Cloud Platform (GCP)

- Microsoft Azure

- Science Soft, etc.

7. Centralized Databases

A centralized database is a particular kind of database that is kept, stored, and maintained in one place. When a user wishes to get data from there, it is safer.

8. Personal Databases

This kind of database is mostly made for a single user and collects and stores data on its system. A personal database is a tiny, one-person database that is usually found on a mobile device or personal computer and is intended to handle data for individual usage. Managing personal data, such as contacts, finances, or notes, is a common application for it. Personal databases are simple to use, lightweight, and don't require complex database administration. Unlike business databases or multi-user databases, they are best suited for single users or minor jobs where only one person interacts with the data. Microsoft Access and SQLite are two examples.

9. NoSQL Databases

A NoSQL database, which was first referred to as non-SQL or non-relational, offers a way to store and retrieve data. In relational databases, this data is modelled using methods other than tabular relations.

Simpler architecture, easier horizontal scalability to machine clusters, and more precise availability control are all features of a NoSQL database. Because NoSQL databases employ different data structures than relational databases by default, some operations in NoSQL databases are quicker. The issue that a particular NoSQL database is intended to address determines its appropriateness. Some people believe that NoSQL databases' data structures are more adaptable than relational database tables(Greeksforgreeks, 2024).

1.3 Key Security Challenges in Cloud Databases

The rules, controls, processes, and technologies that together safeguard Cloud-based systems, data, and infrastructure are collectively referred to as Cloud security. These security measures are intended to protect Cloud-based workloads from cyber-attacks, preserve data privacy, and guarantee regulatory compliance.

A vital component of the Cloud services ecosystem, Cloud security makes sure that user data and apps are safe and functional in a variety of Cloud settings, including public, private, and hybrid Clouds. There is usually a shared responsibility paradigm in the public Cloud, with Cloud customers being accountable for security "in" the Cloud and Cloud providers for security "of" the Cloud.

A complete strategy comprising encryption techniques, customer identification and access management (CIAM), threat detection and response, and ongoing monitoring is necessary for effective Cloud security solutions.

Difference Between Cloud Risks, Threats, and Challenges

When using Cloud services, there is a chance of loss or harm because of a number of things, including vulnerabilities, data breaches, service outages, and noncompliance with regulations. An organization's reputation, financial standing, and operational effectiveness may all be impacted by these hazards.

Cloud threats are particular security problems that have the potential to take advantage of weaknesses in Cloud settings. These dangers, which include insider threats, phishing, and malware assaults, might result in unapproved access, data theft, or system compromise. To create effective preventative strategies, it is vital to comprehend these hazards.

Cloud security difficulties are impediments to Cloud security implementation that make risk and threat prevention and mitigation more challenging. These difficulties could arise from the Cloud environment's complexity, a lack of Cloud knowledge, or inappropriate Cloud environment usage.

Key Cloud Computing Security Challenges

These are some of the main issues influencing Cloud security and solutions for them.

1. Knowledge Gaps

Complexities brought about by Cloud computing necessitate certain knowledge and abilities, which many organizations find difficult to develop internally. The disparity between the IT knowledge that is now accessible and the abilities needed to efficiently manage and protect Cloud settings is growing as a result of the quick evolution of Cloud technologies. This lack of IT know-how may result in less-than-ideal Cloud deployments when security issues are either disregarded or not sufficiently handled.

Additionally, because Cloud services and platforms vary widely, IT workers need to be knowledgeable about a wide range of technologies and be aware of the best practices and security measures for each. Without this knowledge, businesses run the risk of misconfiguring Cloud services, handling access restrictions incorrectly, or neglecting to put crucial security features like encryption and threat detection in place.

How to overcome this challenge:

- To ensure that IT workers stay current with Cloud technology and security best practices, invest in continuous training and certification programs.

- To address knowledge gaps within your company, think about employing or contracting with Cloud security experts.

- Encourage employees to learn new things constantly and provide them with incentives to become proficient in Cloud security.

- Utilize the tools and assistance offered by Cloud service providers, such as their instructional and training materials.

2. Cloud Migrations

A major operation, Cloud migration entails transferring workloads, apps, and data from on-premises data centers to Cloud environments. Because it necessitates a reassessment of current security policies and the deployment of new controls suitable for the Cloud, this process poses a number of security issues. Data may become vulnerable during a migration, particularly if it is not properly planned and carried out.

Businesses need to make sure that the strong security measures offered by their Cloud providers match their own security needs. This frequently entails a thorough evaluation of the Cloud service provider's compliance certifications, data encryption techniques, and security policies.

How to overcome this challenge:

- Before migrating, carry out comprehensive risk assessments and planning to find any possible security vulnerabilities.

- Encrypt all data during the transfer process, both in transit and at rest.

- Collaborate with Cloud service providers that help migration efforts by providing expert services and robust security measures.

- Throughout and after the migration, put strong identity management and access restrictions in place.

- Throughout and after the migration, keep an eye out for security threats to promptly fix any weaknesses.

1. Shadow IT

The use of IT systems, hardware, software, apps, and services without the express consent of the IT department is known as "shadow IT." The availability of Cloud services has increased this problem, making it possible for staff members to quickly implement Cloud-based resources and apps that IT people are not aware of.

The absence of visibility and control over the systems and data being utilized is the main security issue with shadow IT. Without supervision, these unofficial resources could not adhere to the company's security guidelines, putting private data at danger of illegal access or data breaches. Furthermore, shadow IT makes managing data privacy and regulatory compliance more difficult.

How to overcome this challenge:

- Establish a thorough IT governance structure with guidelines for the purchase and use of Cloud services.

- Use Cloud access security brokers (CASBs) to monitor and manage available Cloud services.

- Encourage employees and IT departments to communicate openly in order to comprehend their demands and offer authorized substitutes.

- To find unauthorized services, conduct routine audits and evaluations of Cloud service usage throughout the company.

2. Misconfiguration and Inadequate Change Control

One of the most frequent security problems that businesses encounter is Cloud service misconfiguration. The potential of mistakes is increased by the large number of configuration choices and the simplicity with which modifications may be made in Cloud settings, frequently leaving systems vulnerable to data breaches or unauthorized access.

Any level of the Cloud stack, from database and application settings to network and storage services, is susceptible to misconfigurations. Often, these mistakes stem from a failure to comprehend Cloud security configurations or the intricate relationships among Cloud resources.

How to overcome this challenge:

- To reduce risks, use a least privilege policy and apply stringent access constraints.

- Continuously check for and fix Cloud environment misconfigurations with automated tools.

- Use change control processes to examine and authorize modifications to Cloud setups.

- Perform routine security evaluations and audits to find and fix any possible configuration errors.

3. Insecure Interfaces and APIs

Interfaces and application programming interfaces (APIs) are frequently used to access and control Cloud services and apps, and if not adequately protected, they can be vulnerable spots. Unauthorized access and data leakage are only two of the security risks that Cloud services may face due to insecure interfaces and APIs. When creating or using APIs, developers might not always put security first, which could result in vulnerabilities.

The attack surface is further expanded by the extensive usage of third-party tools and services that communicate with Cloud resources through APIs. The Cloud resources that these third-party components are linked to potentially be accessed by attackers if they are hacked.

How to overcome this challenge:

- Ascertain that robust authentication and encryption procedures are in place to safeguard APIs.

- Make sure that only authorized entities have access by routinely reviewing and updating API access rules.

- Perform routine penetration tests and security evaluations on interfaces and APIs.

- Utilize management tools and API gateways to keep an eye on and regulate API access.

- Reduce the possibility of unwanted access via APIs by using a zero-trust architecture.

4. Software Supply Chain Risks

Cloud settings have serious security concerns due to the intricacy of the software supply chain. When developing and implementing Cloud applications, organizations frequently use a combination of third-party, open-source, and proprietary software components. There is a chance that every link in the software supply chain will create vulnerabilities.

Attacks that target the software supply chain, such inserting malicious code into a popular library, might compromise several Cloud-based apps at once and have far-reaching consequences. A thorough method to screening and keeping an eye on every software component used in Cloud systems is necessary to address software supply chain issues.

How to overcome this challenge:

- Verify and keep an eye on third-party components for security flaws and adherence to regulations.

- Use software composition analysis (SCA) technologies to manage and identify third-party and open-source components.

- Include security checks at every level of the software development life cycle (SDLC) to ensure its security.

- Create a procedure for promptly addressing and resolving vulnerabilities found in the software supply chain.

5. Cloud-Native Malware

Cloud-native malware is developed to target Cloud environments explicitly, taking use of their special features and weaknesses. Cloud-native malware can compromise several accounts and resources by propagating via Cloud services. Cloud-specific capabilities like auto-scaling can be exploited by this kind of malware to spread, or it can leverage Cloud services to attack other targets.

Additionally, without the Cloud service user's awareness, Cloud-native malware can employ the vast processing capabilities of the Cloud for malevolent purposes like bitcoin mining or executing distributed denial-of-service (DDoS) assaults. Specialized Cloud security solutions are frequently needed to detect Cloud-native malware.

How to overcome this challenge:

- Advanced Cloud-specific threat detection and response technologies should be implemented.

- To ensure the safety of data and applications hosted in the Cloud, use Cloud workload protection platforms (CWPPs).

- To keep abreast of new trends in Cloud-native malware, participate in threat information exchange with Cloud providers and trade associations.

- Make sure your incident response strategies account for Cloud-native malware by reviewing and updating them on a regular basis(Aquasec, 2024).

1.4 The Role of Threat Detection and Prevention in Cloud Security

Businesses have been utterly transformed by the advent of Cloud computing, which provides them with scalability, cost-efficiency, and flexibility like never before. Nevertheless, a new set of security concerns is introduced by this change. Cybercriminals are increasingly targeting organizations as they move their sensitive data and mission-critical workloads to the Cloud. It is now critical for Cloud security solutions to incorporate threat intelligence in order to tackle these ever-changing threats. This article delves into the advantages, methodology, and best practices of threat intelligence as it pertains to improving Cloud security.

Understanding Threat Intelligence

Information on actual or prospective dangers to a company is gathered, analyzed, and disseminated through threat intelligence. This data is collected from a variety of places, including as internal security logs, shared threat databases, and open-source data. Our objective is to offer practical insights that will assist organizations in efficiently preparing for, responding to, and anticipating cyber attacks.

The Importance of Cloud Security

Compared to more conventional on-premises installations, Cloud systems are inherently more vulnerable to a wider variety of attacks. Many factors contribute to this:

- **Shared Responsibility Model:** Security is a shared responsibility between clients and Cloud service providers (CSPs). The responsibility for data and application security rests with consumers, even while CSPs safeguard the infrastructure.

- **Dynamic Environments:** Security holes can form in Cloud settings due to their extreme dynamism and the frequent provisioning and de-provisioning of resources.

- **Increased Attack Surface:** Cloud resources are more vulnerable to attacks since they are accessible over the public internet.

- **Data Sensitivity and Compliance:** Strong security measures and regulatory compliance are of the utmost importance for organizations that store sensitive data on the Cloud.

How Threat Intelligence Enhances Cloud Security

- **Proactive Threat Identification:** The capacity of threat intelligence to proactively identify threats is one of its main advantages. Organizations can identify new dangers before they affect their systems by evaluating data from several sources. Threat intelligence, for example, can identify trends in phishing attempts directed at particular sectors, enabling businesses to take preventative action beforehand.

- **Contextualizing Threats:** Threat intelligence helps security teams comprehend the relevance and seriousness of threats by giving the raw data context. For instance, some Cloud deployment types may be more vulnerable to a particular virus version. Organizations may more effectively deploy resources and prioritize their actions by comprehending the threat environment.

- **Enhancing Incident Response:** Threat information is essential to incident response in the case of a security issue. It facilitates the prompt identification of the threat's characteristics, source, and possible consequences. For containment, eradication, and recovery operations, this information is essential. Furthermore, threat intelligence-assisted post-event analysis can assist in improving security protocols to stop similar incidents in the future.

- **Supporting Security Operations Centre (SOC) Teams:** The first line of defense against cyberattacks is SOC teams. These teams are better able to identify, evaluate, and react to threats when they have access to threat intelligence. SOC teams may increase detection capabilities, decrease false positives, and boost overall efficiency by incorporating threat intelligence into their processes.

Types of Threat Intelligence

There are three primary categories of threat intelligence: operational, tactical, and strategic.

- **Strategic Threat Intelligence**

  Strategic threat intelligence offers high-level understanding of the threat environment, including cyber adversary trends, motives, and strategies. Senior management and decision-makers may make well-informed strategic judgements by using this kind of knowledge to comprehend the larger security environment.

- **Tactical Threat Intelligence**

  The methods, tactics, and procedures (TTPs) that attackers employ are the main focus of tactical threat intelligence. Security professionals utilize this highly actionable knowledge to create and carry out targeted defense strategies. IP addresses, domain names, and file hashes linked to malicious activity are examples of indications of compromise (IOCs).

- **Operational Threat Intelligence**

  Operational threat intelligence offers up-to-date information on current threats and assaults. It contains details on threat actors, attack vectors, and ongoing campaigns. This kind of knowledge is essential for quick threat identification and reaction.

Integrating Threat Intelligence into Cloud Security

To effectively leverage threat intelligence in Cloud security, organizations need to integrate it into various aspects of their security architecture. Here are some key areas where threat intelligence can be integrated:

- **Security Information and Event Management (SIEM) Systems:**

  SIEM systems compile and examine data about security events from several sources. Organizations may improve their capacity to identify and address attacks by incorporating threat information feeds into SIEM systems. Threat intelligence may offer more meaning to SIEM data, which facilitates the identification and prioritization of important security incidents.

- **Intrusion Detection and Prevention Systems (IDPS):**

  IDPS keeps an eye on network activity to look for indications of malicious behaviour. By giving IDPS current information on known threats, threat intelligence integration can increase its efficacy. This makes it possible for IDPS to identify and stop threats more quickly and precisely.

- **Endpoint Detection and Response (EDR):**

  EDR solutions concentrate on endpoint-level threat detection and response. Threat intelligence, which offers details on new threats and attack methods, can improve EDR capabilities. This enables EDR systems to identify and address complex threats that can evade conventional security measures.

- **Cloud Security Posture Management (CSPM):**

  CSPM technologies find and fix configuration errors and compliance problems to assist businesses manage and protect their Cloud systems. Organizations may prioritize their remediation efforts by gaining insights into attacks targeting certain Cloud services and configurations through the integration of threat intelligence with CSPM.

- **Identity and Access Management (IAM):**

IAM solutions employ user identities and roles to manage access to Cloud resources. By spotting hacked accounts or unusual login habits, threat intelligence may help IAM policies. This lowers the possibility of unwanted access and allows organizations to establish more efficient access restrictions.

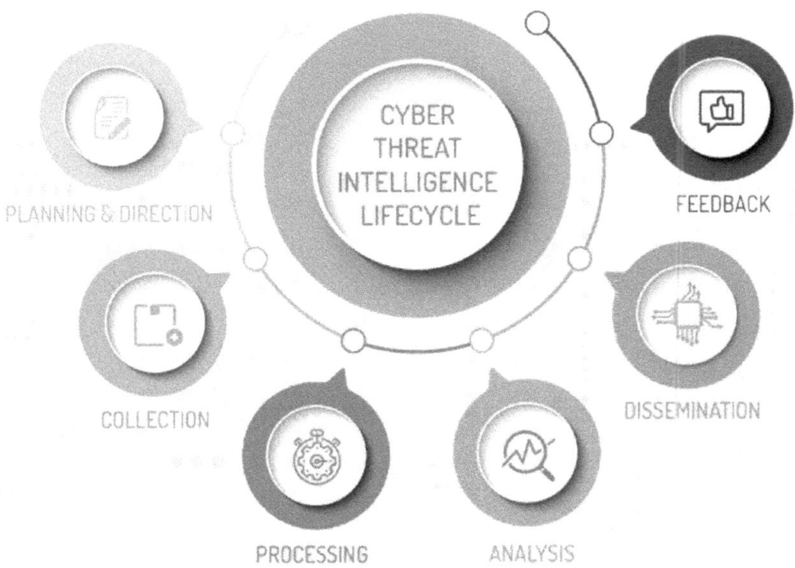

Sources: - *(Muhammad Eissa, 2024)*

Best Practices for Leveraging Threat Intelligence in Cloud Security

Organizations should adhere to these best practices to optimize the advantages of threat intelligence in Cloud security:

- **Establish a Threat Intelligence Program** The first step in incorporating threat information into Cloud security is creating a structured threat intelligence program. The objectives, parameters, and procedures for threat intelligence operations, such as data gathering, analysis, and distribution, should be specified in this program.

- **Collaborate with External Sources** Threat intelligence works best when it integrates data from several sources. Organizations should collaborate with industry organizations, information-sharing platforms, and external threat intelligence providers in order to get a greater range of threat data and insights.

- **Automate Threat Intelligence Processes** Processing threat intelligence data by hand can be laborious and error-prone. Threat intelligence procedures, including data collection, analysis, and reaction, may be made more efficient using automation. Threat intelligence may be automated and integrated with other security tools and workflows using security orchestration, automation, and response (SOAR) systems.

- **Prioritize and Customize Threat Intelligence** Not every organization needs all threat intelligence. Threat intelligence should be prioritized and tailored to the organization's unique requirements and risk profile. This guarantees that security personnel concentrate on the risks that are most pertinent and significant.

- **Continuously Update and Improve** As the threat landscape changes all the time, so too should your attempts to gather threat intelligence. To keep ahead of new threats, update your threat intelligence sources and procedures on a regular basis. Maintain the efficacy and alignment of your threat intelligence program with your security objectives by reviewing and improving it on a regular basis.

Challenges in Implementing Threat Intelligence

Threat intelligence has several advantages for Cloud security, but putting it into practice successfully might present a number of difficulties for enterprises:

1. **Data Overload:** It might be daunting to deal with the sheer amount of threat intelligence data. In order to filter and prioritize pertinent information without becoming overwhelmed by noise, organizations must have the appropriate procedures and tools in place.

2. **Integration Complexity:** It might be difficult to integrate threat intelligence with current security procedures and technologies. In order to prevent vulnerabilities in their security posture, organizations must guarantee smooth integration.

3. **Resource Constraints:** A strong threat intelligence program has to be implemented, which calls for qualified staff and resources. It might be difficult for organizations with little funding to commit the time and energy required for threat intelligence operations.

4. **Keeping Up with Evolving Threats:** The danger environment is ever-changing, with new threats appearing on a regular basis. It takes constant work and attention to detail to stay current with the most recent threat intelligence.

An automated tool for Cloud security and compliance called Cloud Matos assists businesses in better managing and safeguarding their Cloud infrastructures. Cloud Matos enhances Cloud security in a number of ways by utilizing cutting-edge technology like threat intelligence. This is how incorporating threat intelligence into Cloud security may be greatly aided by Cloud Matos:

- **Proactive Threat Detection**

  Integration of Real-Time Threat Intelligence Cloud Matos's security monitoring systems incorporates real-time threat intelligence feeds. It may proactively identify and warn about possible attacks aimed at Cloud settings by continually evaluating threat data from several sources. Because of this, organizations are able to keep ahead of new dangers and take action before they affect the system.

  Automated Threat Recognition The platform employs machine learning algorithms and pre-established criteria to identify dangers through automated procedures. Cloud Matos speeds up the process of identifying possible security problems by automating threat detection, enabling security teams to react more quickly.

- **Contextualizing Threats**

  Increased Exposure and Background Threat actor details, attack paths, and possible consequences are all included in the comprehensive context that Cloud Matos offers for threats that are discovered. Because of this enhanced context, security teams are better able to prioritize their responses by comprehending the importance and relevance of threats.

  Personalization of Threat Intelligence Organizations may use the platform to tailor threat intelligence to their own requirements and risk profiles. Cloud Matos guarantees that security teams concentrate on the most relevant risks to their environment by customizing threat intelligence feeds and warnings.

- **Enhancing Incident Response**

  Automation of Incident Response Workflows for incident response may be automated with Cloud Matos. The platform may immediately start pre-established reaction measures, such blocking malicious IP addresses, isolating impacted resources, and alerting the appropriate staff when a danger is discovered. This automation reduces the possible harm from security issues and speeds up reaction times.

In-depth Analysis of the Incident After an event, Cloud Matos offers thorough analysis and reporting to assist organizations determine the incident's underlying cause, the impact it had, and how well their response efforts worked. In order to enhance future threat detection and response tactics, this study is essential.

- **Supporting Security Operations Centre (SOC) Teams**

  Security Management in One Place A centralized dashboard for overseeing and controlling Cloud security is provided by Cloud Matos. This dashboard gives SOC teams a consolidated picture of their security posture, including incident response operations, security alerts, and real-time threat information. This centralized strategy improves team collaboration and expedites security activities.

  Constant Surveillance of Compliance Additionally, the platform has elements for compliance automation, which guarantees that Cloud environments follow rules and industry standards. Cloud Matos helps organizations prevent security flaws and lowers the risk of regulatory fines by continually checking for compliance.

- **Integration with Existing Security Tools**

  A Smooth Integration Other security products and platforms, including SIEM systems, IDPS, EDR solutions, and CSPM tools, are easily integrated with Cloud Matos. This integration improves overall protection by guaranteeing that threat intelligence is deployed uniformly throughout the organization's security architecture.

  API and Extensibility The platform provides APIs that allow organizations to extend its capabilities and integrate it with custom security workflows and third-party threat intelligence sources. This extensibility ensures that Cloud Matos can adapt to the evolving needs of the organization's security strategy.

- **Overcoming Implementation Challenges**

  Streamlined Implementation Threat intelligence solution deployment in Cloud environments is made easier with Cloud Matos. Threat intelligence integration into current security frameworks is made simpler by its intuitive interface and automated setup procedures. Optimizing Resources Cloud Matos lets businesses maximize their security resources by automating a lot of threat detection and response tasks. Organizations with a small number of security people would especially benefit from this as it allows them to achieve strong security without having to make large budgets or staffing increases.

- **Continuous Improvement**

  Adaptive Education Cloud Matos continually adapts and enhances its threat detection capabilities using machine learning. The platform learns and upgrades its detection algorithms in response to new threats, guaranteeing that it continues to be effective against the most recent attack methods.

  Continual Improvements and Updates The platform is often updated by the Cloud Matos team with new features, threat intelligence feeds, and security improvements. The platform is kept up to date with the most recent security best practices and threat landscapes thanks to these upgrades(CloudMatos, 2024).

1.5 The Importance of Data Protection in the Cloud

The procedures used to ensure that data stored in the Cloud is safe and protected from loss or corruption so that businesses can recover from outages, cyberattacks, and other calamities are known as Cloud data protection. Cloud data protection solutions are becoming more and more necessary as businesses use Cloud storage choices more frequently.

Assessing the organization's degree of risk tolerance, putting in place stringent access restrictions, encrypting data, and separating copies of data from the production environment are some strategies to safeguard Cloud data.

Why is Cloud data protection important?

Structured, unstructured, and semi-structured data—from financial transactions to sales records, customer information, personnel databases, and more—must be protected by businesses.

Reputational and financial disasters may result from data loss or access issues. Because of this, safeguarding the availability and integrity of such data is one of any company's most crucial duties.

This is true regardless of whether a business stores its data remotely on the Cloud or on-site. Procedures are required to protect the data from human mistake, natural calamities, and cybercrime.

Data privacy, integrity, and accessibility

The same tenets of data governance and information security apply to Cloud data security best practices:

- **Data confidentiality:** Only authorized individuals or procedures have the ability to view or alter data. To put it another way, you must guarantee that the information of your company is kept confidential.

- **Data integrity:** Data is dependable, accurate, and authentic, which makes it trustworthy. Implementing regulations or safeguards that stop your data from being altered or erased is crucial in this situation.

- **Data availability:** Data must still be available and accessible to authorized individuals and processes when needed, even if you wish to prevent unauthorized access. You'll have to maintain systems, networks, and devices operating efficiently and guarantee constant uptime.

These three broad pillars, which are sometimes referred to as the CIA triad, stand for the fundamental ideas that underpin any organization's security program or a robust, efficient security infrastructure. One or more of these principles will probably be broken by any attack, vulnerability, or other security issue. For this reason, security experts assess possible threats to an organization's data assets using this methodology.

Challenges of Cloud Data Security

The danger of exposure increases when more data and applications leave a central data centre and migrate away from conventional security measures and architecture. Many of the fundamental components of on-premises data security still exist, but they need to be modified for the Cloud.

Typical issues with data security in hybrid or Cloud contexts include:

- **Lack of visibility.** Businesses don't know what assets are in their inventory or where all of their data and apps are stored.

- **Less control.** Their ability to govern how data is accessed and shared is diminished since apps and data are housed on third-party infrastructure.

- **Confusion over shared responsibility.** Businesses and Cloud providers share responsibility for Cloud security, which may result in coverage gaps if roles and obligations are not well defined or understood.

- **Inconsistent coverage.** Many companies are discovering that multi-cloud and hybrid Cloud better meet their demands, but various providers have varied capabilities and coverage levels, which might result in uneven protection.

- **Growing cybersecurity threats.** Since businesses are still learning how to handle and maintain data in the Cloud, internet fraudsters seeking a large payout find Cloud databases and data storage to be prime targets.

- **Strict compliance requirements.** Businesses are under pressure to adhere to strict privacy and data protection laws, which call for implementing robust data governance and enforcing security standards across various contexts.

- **Distributed data storage.** Lower latency and greater flexibility can be obtained by storing data on foreign servers. However, it can also pose concerns of data sovereignty that might not be an issue if you were running your own data center.(Cloud, 2023).

1.6 The Convergence of Cloud Security and AI

The incorporation of artificial intelligence (AI) and machine learning (ML) into Cloud security is revolutionizing how businesses safeguard their data and infrastructure in the quickly changing digital ecosystem. For companies looking to keep ahead of increasingly complex cyber threats, this convergence is not only a technological breakthrough but also a strategic need. Here, we examine how Cloud security is being revolutionized by AI and ML and why modern businesses must integrate these technologies.

The Role of AI and ML in Cloud Security

1. **Predictive Analytics and Threat Detection:** Predictive analytics is made possible by AI and ML, which improve Cloud security. Large volumes of data are analyzed by these technologies to find trends and abnormalities that might point to possible security risks. AI and ML can predict and reduce dangers before they materialize, thus lowering the attack surface, in contrast to traditional security solutions that respond to known threats.

2. **Automated Incident Response:** The automation of incident response is one of the key benefits of AI and ML in Cloud security. Without human assistance, AI-driven security systems can swiftly assess risks and carry out preset reactions. This capacity to react quickly is essential for minimizing damage during an assault and

guaranteeing that security measures are put in place immediately and efficiently.

3. **Behavioural Analysis:** The behaviour of people and devices inside a network may be observed and learnt from by machine learning algorithms. These systems can identify variations that can indicate a security compromise by creating a baseline of typical behaviour. Behavioral analysis assists in detecting complex cyberattacks and insider threats that elude detection techniques.

Benefits of Integrating AI and ML in Cloud Security

1. **Enhanced Threat Intelligence:** Data from several sources, such as network traffic, security logs, and threat intelligence feeds, may be processed and analyzed using AI and ML. By offering deeper insights into new dangers and attack methods, this thorough research helps organizations remain ahead of hackers.

2. **Scalability:** Cloud infrastructures are naturally scalable, and this ability is further improved by including AI and ML. These technologies are capable of managing the increasing amount of data produced in the Cloud, guaranteeing that security protocols increase with the infrastructure. From startups to major corporations, this scalability is crucial for all types of organizations.

3. **Reduced False Positives:** The high frequency of false positives produced by traditional security systems frequently causes security professionals to become weary of alerts. By improving algorithms based on historical data and real-time analysis, AI and ML increase the accuracy of threat detection. Security teams can concentrate on real threats because of its accuracy, which lowers false positives.

Challenges and Considerations

*   **Data Privacy and Compliance** Although there are many advantages to AI and ML, there are drawbacks as well, including issues with data protection and compliance. Regulations including the CCPA,

GDPR, and HIPAA must be complied with by organisations' AI-driven security solutions. This entails putting in place strong data protection procedures and upholding openness in data processing operations.

- **Integration Complexity:** It may be difficult and requires careful preparation to integrate AI and ML into current Cloud security frameworks. It is imperative for organizations to guarantee that their security personnel has the requisite abilities and know-how to oversee and enhance AI-powered systems. Furthermore, optimizing the advantages of AI and ML requires smooth interaction with existing security procedures and technologies.

- **Future Outlook:** Cloud security's integration of AI and ML is about to advance much farther. More proactive and adaptable security measures that can react instantly to new threats will result from advancements in these technologies. AI and ML will become more and more important in protecting Cloud systems as they develop.

1.7 Chapter Summary

This chapter presented a detailed analysis of Cloud computing and its interaction with databases to give birth to Cloud Databases (Cloud DB) or Database-as-a-Service (DaaS). Cloud computing provides rapid provision of IT resources over the internet without requiring expensive hardware IT resources and infrastructure. Applications that run on Cloud platforms like AWS, Google Cloud, and Microsoft Azure are known as Cloud databases. These platforms let businesses to store, process, and access data while offering benefits like cost savings, scalability, and flexibility. The public, private, hybrid, community, and multi-Cloud Cloud deployment models—all of which have varying degrees of security, flexibility, and control—were also discussed in the chapter. However, the chapter also discusses the purposes and uses of the many types of databases, including relational, NoSQL, and Cloud databases. However, the problem of data security, privacy, and distribution of work load remain the focus especially when adopting Cloud-databases. The chapter goes on to examine subjects of security like the shared responsibility model, migration threats, wrong configurations and Cloud native threats. It provides measures by which these risks can be managed including training, encryption methods, controls to access and access security, and other automated security devices. Last, it discusses how AI and ML can augment Cloud security by providing prescriptive analysis and response coupled with how to overcome integration issues.

Multiple-choice questions (MCQs)

1. **What is the primary focus of cloud computing?**

   a. Managing on-premise hardware

   b. Providing on-demand access to computing resources over the internet

   c. Offering physical storage solutions

   d. Optimizing local database management

2. **What type of system is a cloud database?**

   a. A local server-based system

   b. A remote data storage system managed on the internet

   c. A software-only solution

   d. A hardware-based database system

3. **Which of the following is NOT a key security challenge in cloud databases?**

   a. Data encryption

   b. Secure access control

   c. Increased local hardware maintenance

   d. Multi-tenancy risks

4. **What is the role of threat detection in cloud database security?**

   a. To prevent unauthorized physical access to databases

   b. To monitor and identify suspicious activities or attacks on the cloud system

   c. To limit access to cloud providers' data storage

   d. To ensure regulatory compliance with government standards

5. **Why is data protection important in cloud databases?**

   a. It prevents unauthorized users from deleting data

   b. It safeguards sensitive data from unauthorized access, loss, or corruption

   c. It ensures faster data processing

   d. It minimizes the need for cloud storage space

6. **How does AI contribute to cloud security?**

   a. By eliminating the need for database management

   b. By automating the detection and prevention of threats through machine learning algorithms

   c. By improving cloud providers' network speed

   d. By creating backup copies of cloud data

7. **What is a major security concern related to multi-tenancy in cloud databases?**

   a. Ensuring all users have the same access level

   b. Protecting data from being exposed to other tenants sharing the same resources

   c. Decreasing database performance

   d. Managing physical server locations

8. **Which of the following is a primary technique for protecting cloud database data?**

   a. Increasing server processing speed

   b. Data encryption and secure access protocols

   c. Reducing storage space

   d. Minimizing database queries

9. **In the context of cloud database security, which factor is critical for data integrity?**

   a. Speed of data transfer

   b. Consistent updates and access logs

   c. Availability of cloud storage space

   d. Reducing the number of database queries

10. **How can AI enhance the process of threat detection in cloud databases?**

    a. By conducting manual audits of user activity

    b. By using predictive analytics to forecast potential security threats

    c. By eliminating the need for firewalls

    d. By automatically expanding database capacity

Answers

1	2	3	4	5
B	B	C	B	B

6	7	8	9	10
B	B	B	B	B

Chapter 02

DEEP LEARNING AND MACHINE LEARNING FUNDAMENTALS

2.1 Chapter Overview

This chapter gives an introduction about ML and DL based on their definitions, methods and their potential role in cyber security. The paper starts with defining what ML is, and what its roles are in terms of automating the identification and prevention of threats in various fields. Three variants of ML, namely supervised, unsupervised and reinforcement learning are explained with respect to security with special focus on security issues such as anomaly detection, phishing, and real time threat mitigation.

As a further specialization of ML, deep learning is introducing as a capable method to approach sophisticated data and emerging threats. There is a detailed presentation of the features of neural networks, focusing on the problem of identifying threats with information on the modeling of complex patterns and behaviours. The chapter also discusses the supervised and unsupervised learning methods and then highlight the usefulness of the two approaches in applications such as classification of malware and network security. Reinforcement learning is shown as a dynamic adaptation to implement and automate security processes.

The chapter provides the details of the implementation of ML and DL tasks, the pre-processing and feature selection, model training, that are critical for security system development. Different measures of performance are explained, including precision, recall, and detection rate to give information on how to evaluate the efficiency of different models, particularly when working with imbalanced security data sets.

Finally, how both ML and DL are applied to IDS to enhance the ability to identify and prevent breaches are also discussed. Thus, the chapter concludes with the enumeration of the significance of such technologies in the development of complex, comprehensive, and effective cybersecurity.

2.2 Introduction to Machine Learning (ML)

One form of artificial intelligence (AI) that enables computers to learn without explicit programming is machine learning (ML). This article examines the idea of machine learning, offering a number of definitions and talking about its uses. The skills displayed by learning systems that humans interpret as intelligence are collectively referred to as artificial intelligence. Speech, picture, and video recognition, autonomous objects, natural language processing, conversational agents, perspective modelling, enhanced creativity, intelligent automation, sophisticated simulation, complicated analytics, and prediction are just some of the modern AI's capabilities. Using machine learning and deep learning algorithms, artificial intelligence is used practically in cyber security to identify, anticipate, and react to cyberthreats in real time. This technology is used in information technology, operational technology, the internet of things, control systems, security systems, and the Cloud in general.

Why we need Machine Learning?

Data may be used by machine learning to learn and train and solve/predict complex solutions which cannot be done with traditional programming. It enables us with better decision making and solve complex business problems in optimized time. Applications of machine learning may be found in many domains, including healthcare, finance, education, sports, and more.

Why Machine learning has become essential in every field

1. **Solving Complex Business Problems:**

   It is too complex to tackle problems like Image recognition, Natural language processing, disease diagnose etc. with Traditional programming. Machine learning can handle such problems by learning from examples or making predictions, rather than following some rigid rules.

2. **Handling Large Volumes of Data:**

   Expansion of Internet and users is producing massive amount of data. Machine Learning can process these data effectively and analyze, predict useful insights from them.

   For example, ML can analyze millions of everyday transactions to detect any fraud activity in real time.

   Social platforms like Facebook, Instagram use ML to analyze billions of posts, like and share to predict next recommendation in your feed.

3. **Automate Repetitive Tasks:**

   With Machine Learning, we can automate time-consuming and repetitive tasks, with better accuracy.

   Gmail uses ML to filter out Spam emails and ensure your Index stay clean and spam free. Using traditional programming or handling these manually will only make the system error-prone.

   Customer Support chatbots can use ML to solve frequent occurring problems like Checking order status, Password reset etc.

ML may be used by huge organizations to process vast amounts of data. (like Invoices etc) to extract historical and current key insights.

4. **Personalized User Experience:**

All social-media, OTT and E-commerce platforms uses Machine learning to recommend better feed based on user preference or interest.

Netflix makes movie and TV program recommendations based on your viewing history.

E-commerce platforms suggesting products you are likely to buy.

5. **Self-Improvement in Performance:**

ML models are able to improve themselves based on more data, like user-behavior and feedback. For example,

Voice Assistants (Siri, Alexa, Google Assistant) – Voice assistants continuously improve as they process millions of voice inputs. They adapt to user preferences, understand regional accents better, and handle ambiguous queries more effectively.

Search Engines (Google, Bing) – Search engines analyze user behavior to refine their ranking algorithms.

Self-driving Cars – Self-driving cars use data from millions of miles driven (both in simulations and real-world scenarios) to enhance their decision-making.

Classification of Machine Learning

The four main categories into which machine learning implementations fall are based on the type of learning "signal" or "response" that a learning system can use. These are as follows:

1. **Supervised learning:**

The machine learning job of supervised learning involves using sample input-output pairs to train a function that maps an input to an output. The provided information is labelled. Regression and classification issues are both classified as supervised learning issues.

Example – Consider the following information about patients who walk into a clinic. Each patient is classified as either "healthy" or "ill," and the data includes the patients' age and gender.

Gender	Age	Label
M	48	sick
M	67	sick
F	53	healthy
M	49	sick
F	32	healthy
M	34	healthy
M	21	healthy

2. **Unsupervised learning:**

One kind of machine learning method for making deductions from datasets with input data that lacks labelled answers is called unsupervised learning. The observations in unsupervised learning algorithms are neither classified or categorized. For instance: Examine the following information about patients who walk into a clinic. The information includes the patients' age and gender.

Gender	Age
M	48
M	67
F	53
M	49
F	34
M	21

In terms of learning, it is comparable to the techniques people do to determine that particular items or occurrences belong to the same class, including comparing the degree of resemblance between things.

2.3 Types of Machine Learning Algorithms for Security

2.3.1 Supervised machine learning

A labelled dataset—one in which the objective or outcome variable is known—is used to train the model in supervised machine learning. For example, if data scientists were developing a tornado predicting model, the output would be the actual tornado activity observed for those days, with the input factors being date, location, temperature, wind flow patterns, and more.

Risk assessment, picture identification, predictive analytics, and fraud detection are popular applications of supervised learning.

Several Types of Algorithms

- **Regression algorithms**—Determine the linear correlations between continuous or real inputs (such as temperature and wage) to forecast output values. There are several subtypes of regression algorithms, such as gradient boosting, random forest, and linear regression.

- **Classification algorithms**—Labelling bits of input data allows you to anticipate categorical output variables (such as "junk" or "not junk"). Among the classification techniques are support vector machines (SVMs), logistic regression, and k-nearest neighbors.

- **Naïve Bayes classifiers**—make it possible for big datasets to be classified. Additionally, they belong to a family of generative learning algorithms that simulate the distribution of inputs in a certain class or category. Decision trees, a component of Naïve Bayes algorithms, may support both regression and classification methods.

- **Neural networks**—simulate the functioning of the human brain, with a vast network of interconnected processing nodes that can support functions like speech recognition, picture generation, natural language translation, and image identification.

- **Random forest algorithms**—combine the output from several decision trees to forecast a value or category.

2.3.2 Unsupervised Machine Learning

Unsupervised learning algorithms—Apriorism, principle component analysis (PCA), and Gaussian Mixture Models (GMMs) are examples of techniques that use unlabeled datasets to make conclusions. This allows for exploratory data analysis, pattern detection, and predictive modeling.

Cluster analysis, which use clustering algorithms to classify data points based on value similarity (as in customer segmentation or anomaly detection), is the most popular unsupervised learning technique. Data visualization and dimensionality reduction are made easier by association algorithms, which enable data scientists to find relationships between data items inside huge databases.

K-means clustering—allocates data points into K groups, where K stands for clusters according to their size and degree of granularity, and the data points closest to a specific centroid are grouped under the same category. For market segmentation, document clustering, picture segmentation, and image reduction, K-means clustering is frequently utilized.

Hierarchical clustering—explains a group of clustering methods, such as divisive clustering, which divides a single data cluster according to the differences between data points, and agglomerative clustering, which first isolates data points into groups before merging them iteratively based on similarity until only one cluster remains.

Probabilistic clustering—aids in the resolution of density estimation or "soft" clustering issues by classifying data points according to the probability that they fall into a specific distribution.

The "customers who bought this also bought..." kind of recommendation systems are frequently powered by unsupervised machine learning models.

2.3.3 Self-supervised machine learning

Instead of needing large annotated and/or labeled datasets, self-supervised learning (SSL) allows models to train themselves on unlabeled data. SSL algorithms, often referred to as pretext or predictive learning algorithms, automatically create labels and convert unsupervised issues into supervised ones by learning a portion of the input from another portion. Because the amount of labeled training data required to train models may be extraordinarily huge (and perhaps prohibitively so), these techniques are particularly helpful for professions like computer vision and natural language processing.

Reinforcement learning

A form of dynamic programming known as reinforcement learning, or reinforcement learning from human feedback (RLHF), uses a system of rewards and penalties to train algorithms. An agent acts in a particular environment to accomplish a predefined objective in order to implement reinforcement learning. By rewarding or punishing the agent according to a predetermined measure (usually points), the agent is incentivized to maintain positive behaviours and eliminate negative ones. The agent learns the most effective tactics via practice.

In video game production, reinforcement learning techniques are widely employed to educate robots to do human-like activities.

Semi-supervised learning

A mix of supervised and unsupervised learning is provided by the fifth category of machine learning techniques.

A small labeled dataset and a large unlabeled dataset are used to train semi-supervised learning algorithms, with the labeled data serving as a guide for the learning process of the unlabeled data. In a semi-supervised learning approach, data clusters may be found using unsupervised learning and then labeled using supervised learning.

Semi-supervised machine learning is exemplified by generative adversarial networks (GANs), a deep learning technique that creates unlabeled data by training two neural networks.

Although ML models of any kind may extract insights from company data, their susceptibility to human or data bias necessitates the implementation of ethical AI policies inside organizations.

2.4 Deep Learning Overview and Techniques

What is Deep Learning?

The field of machine learning that is founded on the architecture of artificial neural networks is known as deep learning. To analyze and learn from the incoming data, an artificial neural network, or ANN, employs layers of linked nodes called neurons.

An input layer and one or more hidden layers connected one after the other make up a fully connected deep neural network. The input layer or the neurons in the layer above provide input to each neuron. One neuron's output is used as input by other neurons in the network's subsequent layer, and so on, until the network's output is produced by the last layer. By undergoing a sequence of nonlinear transformations, the neural network's layers enable the network to learn intricate representations of the input data. Because of its success in a range of applications, including computer vision, natural language processing, and reinforcement learning, deep learning artificial intelligence has emerged as one of the most well-known and visible subfields in machine learning today.

2.4.1 Deep Learning Techniques

Convolutional Neural Networks

Convolutional neural networks (CNNs) are a type of artificial neural network designed specifically to evaluate pixel input and are utilised in image processing and recognition. CNNs include image processing, recommender systems, natural language processing, and artificial intelligence (AI) systems that use deep learning to perform generative and descriptive tasks. They often use machine vision, which includes image and video recognition. A neural network is a system of hardware and/or software that is patterned after the functioning of neurons in the human brain. Because they aren't made for image processing, traditional neural networks need to be fed images in smaller pieces. The "neurons" that make up CNN are arranged more like those found in the frontal lobe, which is the area in humans and other animals that processes visual input. The layers of neurons are arranged to cover the whole visual field, avoiding the piecemeal image-processing challenge of traditional neural networks.

Recurrent Neural Networks (RNNs)

The original purpose of RNNs was to help in sequence prediction; the Long Short-Term Memory (LSTM) method is renowned for its adaptability. These networks solely use data sequences with different input lengths as their foundation. The information from its prior state is used as an input value by the RNN for the current prediction. It can therefore help a network achieve short-term memory, which enables efficient handling of stock price changes or other time-based data systems. There are two kinds of RNN designs for issue analysis:

- LSTMs models that rely on memory to forecast data in temporal sequences. They are input, output, and forget.

- For the prediction of temporal sequences based on memory, gated RNNs work well as well. The two gates are Update and Reset.

Generative Adversarial Networks

Generative Adversarial Networks, or GANs, are a subset of generative models that make use of convolutional neural networks and other deep learning methods. The process of automatically recognizing and learning regularities or patterns in incoming data such that the model may be used to generate or output new instances that may have been pulled from the original dataset is known as generative modelling in machine learning.

The generator model, which we train to generate new examples, and the discriminator model, which attempts to classify examples as real (from the domain) or fake (from outside the domain) (generated), are the two sub-models of the supervised learning problem that GANs use to train generative models. To demonstrate that the generator model is generating convincing examples, the two models are trained in an adversarial zero-sum game until the discriminator model is misled around half of the time. It combines two methods from deep learning neural networks. A Discriminator and a Generator. The Discriminator helps differentiate between real and fake data, while the Generator Network creates fake data. Both networks are competitive because the Generator keeps producing fake data that is identical to actual data, while the Discriminator keeps distinguishing between real and fake data. In the event that a picture library is needed, the Generator network would generate simulated data to the real photos. A deconvolution neural network would then be produced. After that, real and fake images would be separated using an Image Detector network. While the generator enhances the creation of phoney images, the detector must enhance the quality of its classification, starting with a 50% chance of accuracy. The total efficiency and speed of the network would increase with such competition.

Deep Reinforcement Learning

Reinforcement learning is the process by which an agent interacts with its environment to alter its state. By interacting with the situation, the agent may watch and respond accordingly, helping a network reach its objective. This network design consists of an input layer, an output layer, and several hidden layers, with the input layer itself representing the environmental state. The idea is founded on repeated efforts to predict the future results of every action taken in a certain situation.

Boltzmann Machines

A symmetrically connected network of units that resemble neurons and make random judgments about turning on or off is called a Boltzmann machine. Boltzmann machines look for intriguing patterns in the training data that point to complex regularities using a simple learning technique. The learning process is slow in networks with several feature detector layers, but fast in "restricted Boltzmann machines" with only one feature detector layer. Multiple hidden layers may be taught rapidly by building restricted Boltzmann machines and using the feature activations of one as the training data for the next. Two kinds of calculations are performed by Boltzmann machines. A cost function is described by the weights on the connections, which are fixed for a search problem. Binary state vectors with low cost function values can therefore be sampled by a Boltzmann machine thanks to its stochastic dynamics. For a learning job, the Boltzmann machine is given a set of binary data vectors and is required to learn how to generate these vectors with a high probability. In order for the data vectors to have low cost function values in comparison to other binary vectors, it must establish weights on the connections. To solve a learning problem, Boltzmann machines generate a lot of little weight modifications, and every update requires them to solve a lot of different search problems.

2.5 Neural Networks and Their Role in Threat Detection

The identification and mitigation of increasingly complex cyber threats are made possible by Artificial Neural Networks (ANNs), which have emerged as a potent tool in the field of cybersecurity. The complexity and frequency of cyberattacks are constantly increasing, making it difficult for traditional rule-based security techniques to stay up. Because of their capacity for learning and adaptation, artificial neural networks (ANNs) have become a flexible way to handle the changing cybersecurity concerns.

This article explores the use of artificial neural networks (ANNs) in cybersecurity, examining its use in a number of areas, including vulnerability assessment, malware analysis, and intrusion detection. It explores how ANNs may be used to improve threat detection and response times, increase the effectiveness of cybersecurity measures, and ultimately fortify an organization's entire security posture through in-depth case studies and pertinent research.

The Fundamentals of Artificial Neural Networks

A subset of machine learning methods known as artificial neural networks (ANNs) are motivated by the composition and operations of the human brain. Similar to the synapses in biological neural networks, they are made up of linked nodes called artificial neurons that process and send information through weighted connections.

An input layer, one or more hidden layers, and an output layer usually make up an ANN's fundamental design. After being received by the input layer, the raw data is processed by the hidden layers, which are where intricate linkages and patterns are discovered. The output layer uses the learnt representations to provide the final predictions or judgments.

Instead than being explicitly programmed with rules, the main characteristic of ANNs is their capacity to learn from data. In order to reduce the error between the expected and intended outputs, this learning process—also referred to as training—involves modifying the weights and biases of the connections between the neurons. The ANN becomes better at identifying patterns and producing precise predictions as training goes on.

ANNs may be divided into a number of different varieties, each having unique architectural features and uses, including feedforward neural networks, recurrent neural networks, and convolutional neural networks. The type of data being processed and the particular problem determine which ANN design is best.

The Importance of Artificial Neural Networks in Cybersecurity

The area of cybersecurity is always changing due to the constant appearance of new threats, weaknesses, and attack methods. In the face of these ever-changing difficulties, traditional security techniques—which frequently rely on rule-based systems and signature-based detection—have grown progressively less effective. Because of their capacity for learning and adaptation, ANNs have shown themselves to be a useful tool for boosting the efficacy of cybersecurity measures.

The capacity of ANNs to identify and react to intricate, unknown dangers is one of its main advantages in cybersecurity. The early identification of new cyber threats is made possible by ANNs' ability to spot minute irregularities and trends in network traffic, user behavior, and system records, in contrast to rule-based systems that depend on preset patterns. This adaptability is especially important when dealing with the continuously changing tactics, methods, and procedures (TTPs) that cybercriminals use.

Additionally, ANNs may be used to automate a number of security-related tasks, including intrusion detection, malware analysis, and vulnerability screening. Organizations may enhance their security posture, lessen the strain for security professionals, and react to attacks more quickly by automating these procedures.

Additionally, ANNs can be utilized for predictive security analytics, enabling security professionals to anticipate and pre-emptively mitigate potential threats. By analyzing historical data and identifying patterns, ANNs can provide valuable insights into the likelihood and potential impact of future cyber-attacks, allowing organizations to allocate resources more effectively and implement proactive security measures.

2.6 Supervised vs. Unsupervised Learning in Threat Detection

Supervised machine

In the training stage of the machine learning model lifecycle, supervised machine learning necessitates tagged input and output data. A data scientist frequently labels this training data at the planning stage before it is utilized to train and evaluate the model. Classifying fresh and unexplored datasets and making predictions are both possible once the model has figured out the link between the input and output data.

This method needs human supervision in at least some cases, which is why it is termed supervised machine learning. The great bulk of the data that is accessible is raw, unlabeled data. In most cases, human engagement is necessary to correctly categorize data that is prepared for supervised learning. Naturally, because it requires vast arrays of precisely annotated training data, this can be a resource-intensive operation.

As a predictive model, supervised machine learning is used to anticipate trends and future changes and categorize unknown data into predefined categories. Supervised machine learning will teach a model to identify objects and the characteristics that categorize them. Supervised machine learning methods are also frequently used to train predictive models. Supervised machine learning models can forecast results from novel and unseen data by identifying patterns between input and output data. This might assist in predicting shifts in home values or consumer buying patterns.

- Frequently, supervised machine learning is employed for:

- Classifying several file formats, including documents, images, and text.

- Finding patterns in training data to predict future trends and results.

ML methods used in supervised learning require labeled datasets for training. Algorithms for supervised learning, which learn from millions of photos and their labels, are commonly used in image-based object detection and categorization. Supervised learning is highly effective at tasks that are clearly specified, but it can only be used when there is a sufficiently large dataset.

To train a very accurate "hot dog or not hot dog" image classifier, for instance, it is necessary to gather pictures of not just hot dogs but, ideally, any other kind of item that may be mistaken for one. Because networks behave differently and are used by many organizations, apps, and users, it is exceedingly difficult to gather a comprehensive dataset with examples of every conceivable scenario in cybersecurity.

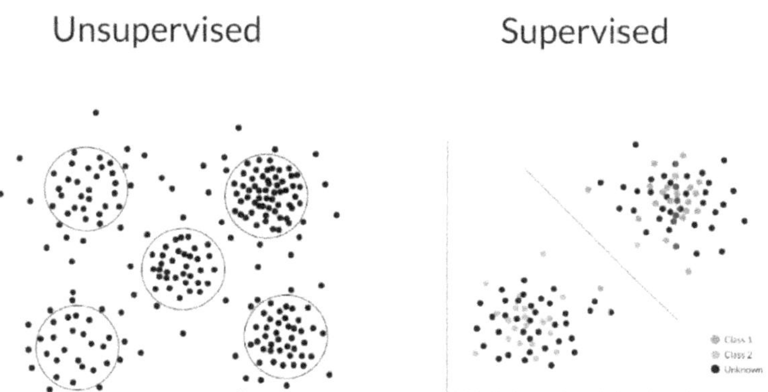

Unsupervised learning

Training models using unlabeled, raw training data is known as unsupervised machine learning. Finding patterns and trends in unprocessed datasets or grouping related data into a certain number of categories are common uses for it. In order to gain a deeper understanding of the datasets, this method is frequently employed at the early exploratory stage.

In contrast to supervised machine learning, unsupervised machine learning takes a more detached approach, as the name implies. The model will handle vast amounts of data efficiently and without human intervention, but a person will specify model hyperparameters like the number of cluster points. Thus, unsupervised machine learning is well-suited to provide answers on hidden patterns and connections in the data itself. However, since there is less human control, unsupervised machine learning's explain ability should be given more thought.

Raw, unlabeled data makes up the great majority of the data that is available. Unsupervised learning is a useful technique for extracting insights from data by clustering data along similar attributes or looking for underlying patterns in datasets. On the other hand, because supervised machine learning requires tagged data, it might be resource-intensive.

- The primary purpose of unsupervised machine learning is to:

- Segment data or group datasets based on feature similarities

- Recognize the connections between various data points, such as automatically generated music suggestions.

- Conduct preliminary data analysis.

Algorithms that can "learn" from a dataset that is completely unlabeled are often referred to as unsupervised learning. Since there is no label or ground truth, it may seem odd that a category of algorithms may learn from the vacuum. Nonetheless, the data still contains a wealth of information, including distribution, trend, and even data itself that may be labelled.

Several applications of unsupervised learning include time-series analysis for stock market or supply chain demand forecast and clustering for market segmentation. Unsupervised learning techniques often operate by assuming realistically how the data in the dataset is distributed. For instance, the algorithm can presume that X has a higher chance of belonging to normalcy if it is highly prevalent in the sample. Without the use of labels, unsupervised learning is highly effective in finding patterns in the data, which may then be utilized to find anomalies or behavioral changes.

Unsupervised learning methods are therefore well-liked by security providers. Additionally, they are very flexible, able to adjust to the unique settings and security protocols of each client.

2.7 Reinforcement Learning and its Application in Security

Even while vulnerability screening technologies have been used extensively for many years, they still have certain drawbacks. For instance, many of these tools are only successful in finding vulnerabilities that have previously been disclosed since they employ a signature-based method to find known flaws. As a result, they are helpless against zero-day exploits, which are assaults that exploit unidentified and undocumented vulnerabilities.

Our AI bot is being trained to identify software code vulnerabilities using reinforcement learning (RL). One kind of machine learning called reinforcement learning teaches an agent to base decisions on a set of rules. The agent may learn and become more accurate over time since it is rewarded for making the right choices and punished for making the wrong ones.

The use of RL for cyber security has several possible advantages.

- **Real-time decision making:** Because RL algorithms are capable of making judgments fast and effectively, they can react to cyber threats instantly.

- **Better threat detection:** RL algorithms may be taught on a sizable dataset of known dangers, which enables them to accurately identify threats that haven't been observed before.

- **Dynamic adaptation:** In a continuously changing cybersecurity scenario, RL algorithms are extremely adaptable and successful because to their ability to adjust to shifting settings and threats.

The use of RL in cyber security is not without its difficulties, though. One of the main obstacles is the dearth of information about actual cyberthreats, which makes it challenging to efficiently train RL algorithms. Concerns exist regarding the ethics and responsibility of AI systems in security and privacy decision-making as well.

Examples of code vulnerabilities that can be found using Reinforcement Learning (RL):

- **Vulnerability scanning**: It is possible to teach an RL-based system to look for vulnerabilities in code and suggest fixes based on the incentives it gets for making the right or wrong choice. Over time, the system may continuously increase its accuracy by learning from its errors.

- **Input validation**: To make sure that user input is free of dangerous payloads, an RL-based system may be taught to check it automatically. When the system properly detects harmful input, it may be rewarded; when it doesn't, it might be penalized.

- **Threat modeling**: A set of predefined security objectives can be used to train an RL-based system to recognize possible dangers in the code and offer mitigation suggestions. The system can learn to recognize dangers and rank them according to their effect and likelihood.

- **Application security**: An RL-based system may be trained to recognize possible security flaws in apps and suggest patches by using the incentives it gets for making the right or wrong choice. Over time, the system's accuracy may be increased by continuously learning from its experience.

2.8 ML and DL in Intrusion Detection Systems

A system that detects intrusions Computer networks and systems may be protected from any type of activity that is deemed unwanted by using intrusion detection systems (IDSs). More conventional rule-based Intrusion Detection Systems (IDS) struggle to keep up with the ever-increasing complexity and number of cyber threats. Deep learning (DL) and machine learning (ML) have been found to have significant effects on increasing the effectiveness of intrusion detection systems. In what follows, we examine the ways in which ML and DL contribute to the development of progressive IDS.

Intrusion Detection System: Brief Introduction

IDS are designed to scan system activity or network traffic for indications of an intrusion, which might include malicious code, illegal conduct, or unauthorized access. IDS are divided into two primary categories:

1. **Signature-Based IDS:** It identifies intruder by analysing network packets based on the library of the different type of attacks. While the approach is effective against the known threats, it performs poorly against zero-day attacks.

2. **Anomaly-Based IDS**: Can detect new types of threats since it is able to compare current behavior with normal / expected behavior. This is where we have the ML and DL methodologies useful.

Therefore, machine learning is a type of artificial intelligence that enables software to identify patterns in data and make decisions without the need for programming. Regarding IDS:

Key ML Techniques Used in IDS:

*   **Supervised Learning:** Support Vector Machines (SVM), Random Forests, and Naive Bayes are examples of machine learning algorithms that are used to analyze and categorize matrices of real network data as either malicious or benign.

*   **Unsupervised Learning**: In the absence of labeled data, procedures such as Principal Component Analysis (PCA) and K-Means Clustering can be used to identify outliers.

*   **Semi-Supervised Learning**: To improve detection or recognition, a little amount of labeled data is combined with a large amount of unlabeled data.

Advantages of ML in IDS

*   Capacity to identify known threats and new threats at that.

*   The non-supervised learning help in the automation of feature extraction and threat classification.

- Its high adaptability to emergent and cariogenic cyber threats.

Challenges

Evidently, the proposed algorithm is highly sensitive to attributes, thus necessitating high-quality data sets for training.

Ability of adversarial attack whereby the attacker changes the input data in a way that will not trigger an alarm.

Deep Learning in IDS

ML; A subset of learning algorithms called "Deep Learning" makes use of neural networks with more than one layer to acquire data patterns without human intervention. It is particularly useful for handling big and sparse data, and thus well-suited for current IDS.

- **Convolutional Neural Networks (CNNs):** Study spatial data and spatial patterns, including packet payloads.

- **Recurrent Neural Networks (RNNs):** Force temporal patterns of events in ordinal data consisting of system logs such as network traffics.

- **Autoencoders:** See effective data representation for anomaly detection.

- **Generative Adversarial Networks (GANs):** To train IDS or to find out adversarial attacks social media synthetic data has to be generated.

Advantages of DL in IDS:

1. The second key advantage has to do with improved capabilities in identifying more complex types of threats, for example APTs.

2. This implies relatively low dependency on feature extraction by hand.

3. Ability to process big and changing data sets.

Challenges

- High computational requirements, which means a considerable demand on the hardware used.

- Interpretability issues commonly described by people as the models being black boxes.

- The need to rely on large labeled datasets for training of new models that will be used in classification.

Applying ML and DL in an IDS

- **Real-Time Threat Detection:** Current live network traffic can be analysed by the ML models to detect and prevent newcomer threats.

- **Malware Classification:** F and M features or the network behavior of files are input to DL models to predict the different types and variants of malware samples.

- **Insider Threat Detection:** In ML, behavioral analysis of insiders can be performed for detecting insiders by pointing out their anomalous behavior.

- **IoT Security:** This is because IoT devices are often targeted by cyber criminals and there are different ML and DL models to protect IoT devices.

- **Fraud Detection:** IDS that joined with ML/DL can identify fraudulent activities of the particular user like corrupting card details or theft of identity. Difficulties and Promotional Outlook

Challenges

Data Quality and Availability: It can be difficult to obtain high-quality labeled datasets for a number of reasons – first, it is an extremely time-consuming process; second; it is much more costly process than unlabelled data; and third, most of the high-quality labeled datasets can be rather limited in size.

- **Evasion Techniques**: Attacker always try to find ways to overcome the ML/DL based IDS thereby creating new methods.

- **Model Generalization:** The key to model robustness from environment and from dataset to dataset.

- **Future Directions:** Federated Learning: Model training together without the exchange of patient data across organizations.

2.9 Data Pre-processing and Model Training

Either data cleaning or data pre-processing and model calibration are among the most important stages in the machine learning process. They make sure the input data is clean, structurally sound, and best importantly, would best serve the training of the model.

1. Data Pre-processing

Pre-processing is a process of data cleaning which is the basic and fundamental step in data mining. This step is to cope with cases, outliers, and gaps, and thus brings data into a more directed form.

Key Steps in Data Pre-processing:

1. **Data Cleaning:** Managing of such cases usually involves strategies such as imputation or deletion of cases.

2. **Remove duplicates:** Place special annotation to correct the errors or the inconsistencies in data.

3. **Data Transformation:** Scale data computed for equal units so that all the values can be measured on the same scale.

4. **Data Integration:** Merge disparate dataset to develop one combined dataset. Co coordinate and manage schema discrepancies and differences in the data structure.

5. **Data Reduction:** One of the powerful ways of Down sampling is by Dimensionality reduction with other methods such as PCA.

6.   **Data Splitting:** The training, validation, and test sets should be created in a typical 7:1:1 or 8:2:2 ratio.

2. Model Training

In order to train the model, the processed data must be run through a machine-learning algorithm. This allows the computer to recognize patterns and relationships in the data that is provided into it. After that, the trained model can be used predict the results of unknown data or data that is not previously used for training.

Steps in Model Training

a. Model Selection

The nature of problem determines which algorithm is used:

- **Regression:** Linear regression, ridge-regular equation, support vector regression etc.

- **Classification:** Classification and Regression trees, bagged trees, neural networks, and log-linear models.

- **Clustering:** K-means, hierarchical, density-based clustering.

- **Deep Learning:** Recurrent layer neural networks, also known as Recurrent Neural Networks (RNNs), for sequential data, and convolutive layer neural networks, also known as Convolutional Neural Networks (CNNs), for picture data.

b. Training Process

The core of model training involves:

- **Initialization:** Designate values for parameters starting the particular model – for example weights of neurons in neural networks.

- **Forward Propagation:** The model works on input data and produces predictions upon which something is based.

- **Loss Calculation:** Estimate the deviation of the target from values assumed by the model using a loss function like cross-entropy or MSE.

- **Backward Propagation:** Compute gradients of the loss regarding the model parameters.

- **Optimization:** Modify several parameters for usages of algorithms like gradient descent or even Adam optimizer.

c. Regularization

Regularization adds a penalty to the loss function for complicated models, preventing overfitting:

- **L1 Regularization (Lasso):** Encourages high dimensionality on characteristics.

- **L2 Regularization (Ridge):** Discourages large weights.

- **Dropout:** Part of neurons are dropped when training to enhance generalization in neural networks.

d. Hyperparameter Tuning

These are parameters that are not part of the model but are utilized throughout the model's training phase. Techniques to optimize them include:

- **Grid Search:** A technique which involves a systematic search of the parameter space.

- **Random Search:** It is a method by which the parameter space is sampled randomly.

- **Bayesian Optimization:** Approaches the problem of hyperparameter optimization using probabilistic models.

e. Cross-Validation

Partition the data into k subsets in order of enrolment of the participants to confirm each subsequent model. To do k-fold cross validated, train on k –1 part and validate on the remaining part (< |k | >). data into a machine learning algorithm so that it may discover correlations and trends. The results of fresh, unknown data are then predicted using the trained model.

f. Early Stopping

The overall idea is to pay attention to the validation performance during the training step. Quit the training when the performance fails to increase in order to avoid over training.

Post-Training Steps

a. Model Evaluation

Test the model on unseen test data using metrics like:

- **Classification:** These include Mean accuracy of all folds, f1 f-score, precision, recall-ROC.
- **Regression:** RMSE, MAE, R^2.

b. Error Analysis

Break things down in order to optimize them, for example whether there are certain cases that were classified in a wrong manner or if there is a high residual risk.

c. Model Deployment

Use the trained model in production or different other systems available. Basic, Monitoring must be done to make sure the model develops and performs well on real data.

d. Model Retraining

Now and then, retrain the model using the new data in order to continually improve its efficiency, particularly in ever-changing situations.

Security domains such as intrusion detection, malware identification, phishing identification, and fraud identification need to compare the ML and DL models. Because these domains usually contain skew data and evolving threats, the proper choice of evaluation metrics helps prevent developing ineffective models.

Main Difficulties when Assessing the Security Model

- Class Imbalance: For security datasets, a large number of instances are often benign than they are malicious thus calling for the use of other better measures of accuracy.

- High Stakes: False negatives which means failing to detect a threat result in a breach while false positives are when the SE marks an event as malicious which in fact it is not creates inconveniences.

- Dynamic Nature of Threats: There are still challenges such as new attacks, improvement of attacks and identification of unknown types of patterns.

- Real-Time Performance: Almost all security tasks demand models to run in real time, that is, without flaws.

Common Evaluation Metrics

a. Often, measures of Classification tasks are used.

- **Confusion Matrix Components:** The first necessary step is identification of true positive (real threats) or true negative (nonthreat events), false positive or false negative.

- **Accuracy:** Estimates how often predictions are accurate. Although, it is an effective method and may mislead when the data set is imbalanced.

- **Precision:** Meaning shows how many of the threats predicted really exist. It is important when false positives are expensive, for instance when trying to detect fraud.

- **Recall (Sensitivity):** Evaluates the model's capacity of identifying all true threats. This is very important so as to avoid cases where something malicious is performed and not picked by the system.

- **F1-Score:** A good measure for both precision and recall, hence it can be used when false positive results and false negative results are important both.

- **AUC-ROC (Area Under the Curve for Receiver Operating Characteristic):** Determines the kind of performance of the model in the differentiation of between malicious and benign activities depending on the given thresholds.

- **AUC-PR (Area Under the Curve for Precision-Recall):** Especially important for cases with an unequal number of records of different classes as it measures the performance on the positive class.

- **False Positive Rate (FPR):** Measures how often an organization deems an event harmless when it is actually threatening.

- **False Negative Rate (FNR):** Indicates how many threats are not detected by the model, which is important for security-related activities when risk cannot be tolerated.

b. Metrics for Regression Tasks

In cases such as predicting the severity of security breaches or even anomaly scores, It is often possible to employ measures like Mean Absolute Error (MAE), Mean Squared Error (MSE), and R-Squared. Mean absolute error (MAE), mean squared error (MSE), and $R2$ are examples of regression metrics that are frequently used to estimate the severity of security events or anomaly scores. These are based on how near estimates are to actual measurements.

New Methods in Security Technologies

- **Detection Rate (DR):** Illustrates how accurately it determines suspicious deeds and is frequently contrasted with gross examination

- **False Alarm Rate (FAR):** Suggests how many of the benign events are sampled incorrectly by the system as being malicious.

- **Matthews Correlation Coefficient (MCC):** A single metric for imbalanced datasets directly related to all parts of the confusion matrix.

- **Threat Score (TS) or Critical Success Index (CSI):** Normally applied in determining the performance of the approach in accurate detection of the malicious activities and simultaneously take into account the frequencies of false positives and false negatives.

Evaluation Techniques

- **Cross-Validation:** Splits data into different parts that is used both for training the model and evaluate its performance and applicability.

- **Stratified Sampling:** Retains the ratio of the benign and the malignant cases between the training and testing sets particularly for those cases with a skewed distribution.

- **Real-Time Testing:** Checks the model's fitness for evaluating live data streams based on latency and throughput.

- **Adversarial Testing:** Just as we have test data of one distribution to check generalization, expose models to manipulated data or adversarial attacks.

Commodity Metric Selection according to Appropriate Uses

- **Intrusion Detection Systems (IDS):** Accurate measurements such as recall, detection rate, the false alarm rate, and the F1 score are privileged in order to minimize threats slipping through undetected while keeping the alert rate low enough as to not overwhelm system administrators.

- **Malware Classification:** As previously discussed; precision and recall is fundamental to achieving a balance in identifying malicious code while at the same time avoiding false alarms that are very common.

- **Phishing Detection:** AUC-ROC and precision minimize errors where authentic messages are classified as phishing.

2.10 Chapter Summary

This chapter introduces the ideas of ML and DL and their basic concepts, including their proffered security applications are well elucidated. This is followed by a brief description of the ML as the fundamental tool for analyzing and combating contemporary cyber threats. More specifically, the chapter gives an overview of the three main categories of ML algorithms—supervised, unsupervised, and reinforcement learning—and how best they can be employed in security tasks, including threat identification, anomaly detection, and real time decision making.

This paper provides an elaborate discussion on deep learning while positing that the neural network forms the backbone of the process in handling intricate data. convolutional and the recurrent neural networks are presented as effective tools for threat identification and threat prediction in open areas. In the chapter, the author differentiates between supervised and unsupervised learning and how each applies to security circumstances such as identifying malware or a network anomaly. Reinforcement learning is also considered for its applicability in real-life, adaptive security solutions including security response automation.

Some of the more specific topics in the development of ML and DL systems are discussed, to include data pre-processing and model training for that data, with the focus being on the quality of the data and how it should be prepared for the development of a proper model. Chapter 4 focuses on the evaluation measures especially for imbalanced security datasets and it also introduced other measures Such as the F1-score, detection rate, false alarm rate, accuracy and recall.

Lastly, the chapter examines the combination of ML and DL in implementing IDS and evidence how these technologies are disrupting the security landscape. But it concludes that accuracy, scalability, and adaptability are factors that need to be considered well when using ML and DL models in cybersecurity.

Multiple-choice questions (MCQs)

1. **What is the primary goal of Machine Learning (ML)?**

    a. To develop software that can run without any data

    b. To enable computers to learn from and make decisions based on data

    c. To manually code every decision-making process

    d. To design faster hardware for databases

2. **Which type of machine learning algorithm is most commonly used in threat detection systems?**

    a. Linear regression

    b. Classification and clustering algorithms

    c. K-means clustering

    d. Principal component analysis (PCA)

3. **What is deep learning primarily used for in the context of threat detection?**

    a. Managing the user interface of security systems

    b. Automating the detection of complex patterns in large datasets

    c. Minimizing network traffic

    d. Encrypting sensitive data

4. **What role do neural networks play in threat detection systems?**

   a. They act as databases for storing threat data

   b. They process and analyze large datasets to detect anomalous behaviors or attacks

   c. They monitor hardware performance only

   d. They handle encryption and decryption of security protocols

5. **In supervised learning, what is the main difference compared to unsupervised learning?**

   a. Supervised learning requires labeled data, while unsupervised learning does not

   b. Supervised learning works with unlabeled data, while unsupervised learning uses labeled data

   c. Unsupervised learning is more accurate than supervised learning

   d. There is no difference between supervised and unsupervised learning

6. **What is a key application of reinforcement learning in security systems?**

   a. To continuously learn from feedback and improve decision-making for security protocols

   b. To automate the encryption process for sensitive data

   c. To store security logs in the cloud

   d. To manage hardware resources in security systems

7. **How do Machine Learning (ML) and Deep Learning (DL) techniques benefit Intrusion Detection Systems (IDS)?**

   a. By improving the accuracy of threat identification and reducing false positives

   b. By storing more data

   c. By encrypting sensitive information

   d. By monitoring hardware performance

8. **What is the main goal of data pre-processing in machine learning?**

   a. To reduce the size of datasets

   b. To clean and transform raw data into a format suitable for model training

   c. To store the data in cloud databases

   d. To perform data backups

9. **What is the purpose of model training in machine learning and deep learning?**

   a. To determine the hardware specifications for running the model

   b. To optimize the model's performance by adjusting its parameters based on training data

   c. To manually inspect the model's outputs

   d. To store models for future use

10. **Which of the following evaluation metrics is commonly used to assess the performance of machine learning and deep learning models in security applications?**

    a. Speed of data transfer

    b. Accuracy, precision, recall, and F1 score

    c. Power consumption

    d. Hardware utilization

Answers

1	2	3	4	5	6	7	8	9	10
B	B	B	B	A	A	A	B	B	B

Chapter 03

THREAT DETECTION USING MACHINE LEARNING AND DEEP LEARNING

3.1 Chapter Overview

The chapter offers a thorough examination of unsupervised learning methods for cybersecurity zero-day threat detection, focusing on their ability to identify previously unknown threats without the need for labeled data. It explains the significance of zero-day attacks, which exploit undiscovered vulnerabilities, and how these abnormalities may be found using unsupervised learning in a variety of fields, such as industrial control systems, web security, and network intrusion detection. Important unsupervised learning methods including autoencoders, dimensionality reduction, and clustering are covered in this chapter, and isolation forests, and discusses their effectiveness in anomaly detection. It also discusses these techniques' drawbacks, such as their high false positive rates, the need for adaptability to evolving threats, and computational complexity. Furthermore, the chapter highlights advancements in hybrid models, meta-learning, and zero-shot learning as future directions to improve detection capabilities. Additionally, it explores real-time detection systems driven by deep learning and machine learning and highlights the significance of feature selection in optimizing machine learning models.

The integration of these technologies in real-time applications, including case studies in network security, healthcare, and autonomous cars, is covered in the chapter's conclusion.

3.2 Threat Detection Mechanisms

Advanced threat detection and response counters cyber threats with modern technologies, methodologies, and capabilities. Both automated, passive tools and more active, human-cantered strategies are important to SaaS Threat identification and mitigation:

Automated/passive tools

- **Machine learning algorithms and AI.** In order to identify sophisticated threats in real time, machine learning algorithms examine vast amounts of past data. This enables them to increase the threat detection process' precision and effectiveness.

- **Endpoint detection and response (EDR).** Advanced threat detection tools often integrate with EDR solutions. These monitor endpoint behavior in real-time, uncover suspicious activities, and facilitate forensic analysis to detect threats and enable a rapid response to endpoint-related security incidents.

- **Automated responses to security incidents.** Use available tools to speed the organizational response to cyber threats, including: quarantine/isolation for infected or compromised endpoints and systems, blocking malicious IP addresses, and triggering remediation workflows based on set criteria.

- **Integration with security orchestration, automation, and response (SOAR).** Integrated SOAR platforms allow more efficient threat response at scale.

Active/human-cantered strategies

- **Behavioral analysis techniques.** Identifying abnormal patterns and deviations in account behavior, network traffic, application activity, and system processes enables the detection of compromise and threats that risks that could be overlooked by conventional signature-based methods.

- **Threat hunting.** This proactive search for concealed dangers and indications of network penetration necessitates the use of specialized technologies, threat intelligence, and human knowledge.

- **Deception technologies.** These technologies such as honeypots, decoy assets, and breadcrumbs lure attackers into engaging with fake systems and collect valuable threat intelligence. Deception can help detect intrusions early, gather information about attacker tactics, and divert adversaries away from critical assets.

- **Threat intelligence fusion.** Aggregated threat intelligence from internal telemetry, open-source intelligence (OSINT), industry feeds, and proprietary feeds provides a more thorough assessment of the danger environment.

How Does Threat Detection Work?

Comprehensive enterprise threat detection combines technologies and human expertise to continuously monitor for indicators of compromise to instantly recognize, evaluate, and lessen any risks:

- **Continuous monitoring.** Real-time threat detection is fueled by an ongoing flow of data from several sources across the IT environment, such as network traffic, logs, endpoint activity, user behaviour, and external threat intelligence feeds.

- **Active threat detection techniques.** Signature-based anomaly detection, behavior analysis, machine learning, and threat intelligence all help identify potential threats and existing security issues, whether they were previously known or are novel.

- **Event correlation and threat detection analysis.** IT teams are able to ascertain the severity, context, and possible influence on the organizational security posture of threats by analyzing the correlation between identified threats and alarms.

- **Incident investigation.** Upon detecting threats, these systems initiate a process to investigate the nature and scope of the issue. Analysts and/or managed threat detection tools conduct forensic and root cause analyses and gather evidence to assess the extent of the compromise.

- **Response and mitigation.** Determine the source and nature of any threats including all appropriate responses. Responding to threats may include isolating or terminating compromised systems or processes, applying security patches or updates, blocking malicious IP addresses or domains, and restoring affected data from backups. Additionally, eradicating attacker artifacts, account recovery, rotating compromised credentials.

- **Adaptive security controls.** Solutions for real-time threat detection often dynamically adjust security policies, configurations, and controls based on real-time risk assessments. This helps to proactively strengthen defense and minimize the attack surface.

- **Intelligence integration.** Cloud threat detection and response systems integrate with threat intelligence feeds to enrich analysis and improve detection accuracy. Threat intelligence offers valuable context about known threats, attacker tactics, techniques, and procedures.

- **Continuous threat detection and improvement.** To succeed, the process should be iterative, involving continuous improvement based on careful analysis of past security incidents and emerging threat trends.

What Are 4 Methods of Threat Detection?

Although there are many methods for seeing and addressing possible security risks and malevolent activity in the IT environment, they may be broadly divided into four threat detection categories:

- **Signature-based detection.** Comparing observed data such as network traffic patterns against predefined rules or patterns of malicious activity to identify threats is effective for detecting recognized attack tactics and viruses. But it can have trouble identifying new or altered threats that don't fit the signatures that are already there.

- **Anomaly-based detection.** This finds variations in the IT environment's typical behaviour or baseline patterns that might point to a security risk. Although insider threats, zero-day assaults, and previously unidentified threats can be found with anomaly threat detection management, as environments get more sophisticated and overall account use patterns change over time, it may also produce false positives.

- **Behavior-based detection.** This kind of monitoring for threats detects lateral movement, privilege escalation, and data exfiltration—issues that may evade other defense—but requires advanced analytics and deep contextual understanding of typical user, application, and system behavior.

- **Threat intelligence-based detection.** File hashes linked to cyber threats or IP addresses or domains are examples of known malicious entities that may be proactively blocked with the use of external feeds and signs of compromise. Threat intelligence-based detection supports other detection methods, enriching security alerts with contextual information and enabling proactive threat hunting.

How to Detect Security Threats

What is threat detection technology and how does it ensure that vulnerabilities and attacks are mitigated? Because SaaS threat detection is a systematic, repeatable, verifiable process, it reliably mitigates security challenges in an organizational IT environment. Here are some specific ways that Cloud threat detection works to detect both known and novel threats:

- **Continuous monitoring tools and technologies.** These enable continuous network, system, application, and data monitoring.

- **Data collection and aggregation tools.** These offer visibility into the environment and include network traffic logs, system logs, firewall logs, endpoint telemetry, user activity logs, and external threat intelligence feeds.

- **Varied Cloud security threat detection techniques.** Approaches should detect both known and previously unseen attacks, using threat intelligence-based detection, behaviour analysis, machine learning, anomaly detection, and signature-based detection.

- **Alert generation.** When security tools detect security threats, they create notifications or alerts to notify incident response teams. The detected incident, its intensity, pertinent context, and suggested course of action are usually all included in these alerts.

- **Alert triage and investigation.** Security analysts conduct forensic analysis, correlate related events, and assess the potential risk detected threats pose to organizational security posture.

- **Incident response process.** Confirmed security incidents demand a controlled and documented response that can contain and eradicate threats. To isolate impacted systems, this might entail putting security controls in place, applying patches or updates to remediate vulnerabilities, blocking malicious activities, and restoring affected data from backups.

Threat Detection in Cyber Security

Cyber security threat detection is similar to the concepts discussed above, but focuses specifically on responding to security in the digital realm.

Cybersecurity threat detection differs from and aligns with the broader threat detection context in some of ways:

- **Digital context.** Cyber threat detection specifically addresses digital environments.

- **Cyberattacks.** This includes any type of unauthorized attempt to gain access or compromise of the availability, availability, or secrecy of digital assets.

- **Digital data.** Data from several sources, including user activity, application, and network traffic records; endpoint telemetry, is necessary for the detection of cyber threats; and external threat intelligence feeds.

- **Detection techniques.** Cyber threat detection employs a combination of detection techniques, as described above.

- **Automated analysis.** Using machine learning algorithms and sophisticated analytics, cyber security operations frequently include the automated examination of massive amounts of data. that rapidly process digital data to identify malicious activity and generate notifications to prompt further action.

- **Human expertise.** Human experts know how to detect cyber threats and remain essential for interpreting alerts, assessing the gravity and consequences of identified threats, and making informed decisions about response actions.

- **Integration with incident response.** Detected threats trigger these workflows, which mitigate the consequences of security lapses and prevent future incidents.

3.3 Identifying Anomalies in Cloud Databases

Anomaly detection in Cloud databases is vital for preserving data security and integrity, and optimal performance. Building upon the foundational approaches previously discussed, here are additional insights and best practices to enhance your anomaly detection strategies:

Advanced Techniques:

- **Deep Learning Models:** Recurrent neural networks (RNNs) and autoencoders are two examples of deep learning algorithms that may be used to capture intricate, non-linear correlations in data, enhancing the identification of minute abnormalities. These models are particularly effective in high-dimensional datasets common in Cloud environments.

- **Hybrid Approaches:** Increasing detection accuracy may be achieved by combining machine learning and statistical approaches. For instance, integrating clustering algorithms with supervised learning models allows for the identification of both known and unknown anomalies.

Best Practices:

- **Data Aggregation:** Aggregate time-series data into regular intervals (e.g., hourly, per-minute) to guarantee that it is distributed equally. The performance of anomaly detection methods is improved by this preprocessing step.

- **Regular Model Evaluation:** To adjust to changing data patterns, evaluate and update your models often. Accuracy may be gradually increased by putting in place a feedback loop where identified anomalies are examined and utilized to retrain models.

- **Scalability Considerations:** As the volume of data grows, ensure that your anomaly detection system can scale accordingly. Leveraging distributed computing frameworks and optimizing algorithms for parallel processing can help manage large datasets efficiently.

Challenges and Mitigation:

- **High Dimensionality:** Cloud databases often contain vast numbers of features, making the process of detecting anomalies computationally demanding. This problem can be lessened by using dimensionality reduction techniques, including Principal Component Analysis

(PCA), which reduce the dataset while preserving important information.

- **False Positives/Negatives:** Balancing sensitivity and specificity is crucial to minimize false alerts. Regularly tuning model parameters and incorporating domain knowledge can help achieve this balance.

Tools and Resources:

- **Python Libraries:** Utilize libraries such as PyOD to discover anomalies in a scalable manner. PyOD incorporates optimizations like multi-processing for quicker model fitting and supports both supervised and unsupervised detection on multivariate time series data.

- **Cloud Provider Services:** Leverage built-in anomaly detection features offered by Cloud providers. For example, using machine learning methods, AWS's CloudWatch Anomaly Detection enables you to continually examine system and application information, identifying anomalies in real-time.

Integrating these advanced techniques and adhering to best practices, organizations can enhance their anomaly detection capabilities in Cloud databases, leading to improved data quality and system reliability.

3.4 Classification Algorithms for Threat Identification

Classification algorithms are essential tools in the realm of threat detection, particularly in identifying and categorizing potential security threats within various systems. These algorithms leverage patterns and features extracted from data to assign specific labels or categories, enabling the detection of anomalies or malicious activities. Below, we explore the foundational aspects of classification algorithms in the context of threat identification:

Overview of Classification in Threat Detection

In order to predict the category of new data, a model is trained on labelled data using supervised machine learning techniques, unseen data. In the context of threat identification, this translates to recognizing patterns associated with benign and malicious activities. Examples include distinguishing normal network traffic from intrusion attempts or categorizing emails as spam or phishing attempts.

Commonly Used Classification Algorithms

Various algorithms have proven effective for threat identification, each with unique strengths tailored to specific types of threats or datasets:

- **Logistic Regression:** A statistical technique frequently applied to binary classification issues, such determining if a file is harmful or not.

- **Decision Trees:** Provide interpretable models by mapping decision-making paths based on input features. Effective for identifying structured threats with distinct patterns.

- **Random Forests:** An ensemble approach that reduces overfitting and increases classification resilience by integrating many decision trees.

- **Support Vector Machines (SVM):** Work well for detecting threats in high-dimensional feature spaces by finding an optimal hyperplane for classification.

- **k-Nearest Neighbours (k-NN):** It is appropriate for smaller datasets as it classifies risks according to how closely data points resemble their closest neighbors.

- **Naïve Bayes:** A probabilistic classifier efficient for text-based threats like email spam detection, leveraging conditional probabilities.

- **Neural Networks:** Highly effective for complex threat detection tasks, such as identifying sophisticated cyberattacks, especially when combined with deep learning techniques.

Applications of Classification Algorithms in Threat Detection

Classification algorithms find applications in a variety of threat identification scenarios, including:

- **Intrusion Detection Systems (IDS):** Identifying harmful or regular network traffic.

- **Email Filtering:** Identifying phishing emails or spam.

- **Malware Detection:** Distinguishing between benign and malicious software.

- **Anomaly Detection in Cloud Databases:** Classifying activities as normal or suspicious in large-scale Cloud environments.

Challenges in Classification for Threat Detection

Despite their effectiveness, classification algorithms face challenges in threat detection:

- **Imbalanced Data:** Threat-related datasets often have a disproportionate number of benign versus malicious samples, affecting model performance.

- **Evolving Threat Patterns:** Cyber threats constantly evolve, necessitating retraining and updating of models to remain effective.

- **False Positives and Negatives:** Misclassification can lead to overlooking threats or raising unnecessary alerts, impacting system reliability.

- **Feature Selection:** The accuracy and effectiveness of the model may be greatly impacted by determining which features are most essential for categorization.

Future Directions

To address the challenges and enhance effectiveness, integrating hybrid approaches such as combining machine learning with rule-based systems or leveraging ensemble methods can be beneficial. Furthermore, real-time threat detection can be improved by incorporating adaptive learning techniques that allow classification models to update dynamically in response to emerging threats. Employing classification algorithms effectively, Organisations may boost overall security measures by greatly improving their capacity to recognize and neutralize threats.

3.5 Using Natural Language Processing (NLP) for Threat Detection

In today's digital environment, cyber security has become increasingly important, affecting both individuals and companies. With data quantities and complexity continuing to rise, traditional security methods might not be sufficient to identify and stop emerging threats. Natural language processing, or NLP, now comes into play. By examining and drawing conclusions from textual input, the artificial intelligence field of natural language processing (NLP) gives security professionals strong tools to improve cyber defenses. Numerous techniques and algorithms that come under this general category enable computers to read, understand and even produce their own natural language content.

Cybersecurity relies heavily on natural language processing (NLP), especially when dealing with unorganized data. Emails, social media posts, and online forum threads are some of instances of unstructured data, and text documents that lack a predetermined framework or organization. Natural language processing (NLP) is important for cyber security because it can sift through this kind of unstructured textual data, find patterns, and reduce risks. Cyber security experts may use natural language processing (NLP) to sift through documents, social media postings, emails, and other forms of unstructured textual data in search of patterns and insights.

Applications of NLP in Cyber Security

Let's talk about some of applications of natural language processing (NLP) approaches for identifying fraudulent material.

- **Identifying phishing emails:** Through text analysis, NLP may be used to detect phishing emails. NLP, for instance, may be used to detect emails that contain specific terms or phrases, such "urgent," "important," or "click here," that are frequently used in phishing emails.

- **Identifying phishing websites:** Additionally, by examining the website's text, NLP can be used to detect phishing websites. NLP can be used, for instance, to find websites that use terms or phrases like "secure," "verified," or "official," which are frequently found in phishing websites.

- **Training machine learning models:** Machine learning models that identify phishing may also be trained using natural language processing (NLP). A collection of phishing emails and websites may be used to train machine learning algorithms. The model may be used to recognize fresh phishing emails and websites after it has been taught.

- **Identifying suspicious links:** Untrustworthy links in emails and webpages can be found using natural language processing (NLP). NLP, for instance, may be used to find URLs that contain terms or phrases like "bank," "credit card," or "password," which are frequently used in phishing attempts.

- **Identifying typos and grammatical errors:** Grammatical and typographical mistakes are frequently seen in phishing emails and websites. These mistakes, which may indicate that the email or website is fake, can be found using natural language processing (NLP).

- **Identifying unusual behavior:** Unusual behaviour in emails and webpages may be detected with NLP. NLP, for instance, may be used to recognize emails that come from unknown senders or that have unexpected attachments.

These language-based detection methods improve people's and organizations' overall cybersecurity posture by bolstering a complete defense against phishing assaults in conjunction with other security measures like anti-spam filters and user education.

Key NLP Techniques in Cyber Security

In order to process and derive insights from text input, Natural Language Processing (NLP) combines rule-based and machine-learning methodologies.

- **Named Entity Recognition (NER):** A basic NLP method called NER finds and extracts certain entities from text, including names, places, organizations, and dates. When it comes to cyber security, NER is essential for identifying and removing sensitive data. By automatically identifying personally identifiable information (PII) in emails or postings on social media, NER contributes to user privacy protection and data protection law compliance.

- **Sentiment Analysis:** Finding the sentiment or opinion—whether positive, negative, or neutral—expressed in a text is the goal of sentiment analysis. Sentiment analysis is a useful tool in the field of cyber security for examining customer evaluations, comments, and feedback about security goods and services. Organizations can learn about possible weaknesses, dangers, or opportunities for development by analyzing user sentiment.

- **Part-of-Speech (POS) Tagging:** The technique of giving words in a phrase grammatical tags is known as POS tagging. This method makes it easier to comprehend the text's grammatical structure, which is useful for spotting security risks. Cyber security experts can identify questionable patterns, including command-like phrases or improper language, that can point to malicious intent or social engineering attempts by examining the part of speech of each word.

3.6 Unsupervised Learning for Zero-Day Attack Detection

It is quite difficult to identify zero-day attacks, or exploits that target vulnerabilities that have not yet been discovered, in the quickly developing field of cybersecurity. The inability of conventional signature-based detection techniques to recognize these new dangers frequently calls for the creation of more intelligent and flexible detection systems. Unsupervised learning, a subfield of machine learning that finds patterns in data without labels, has become a viable solution to this problem.

Zero-Day Attacks

Zero-day attacks take use of flaws that security experts and software makers are unaware of at the time of the assault. Developers have 0 days to fix and patch the vulnerability, as the phrase "zero-day" indicates. Because they may get past conventional security measures and do serious harm before being discovered and fixed, these assaults are very dangerous.

Unsupervised Learning in Cybersecurity

Unsupervised learning algorithms analyze data to detect hidden patterns or intrinsic structures without prior labeling. In cybersecurity, these algorithms are instrumental in identifying anomalies that may indicate malicious activities, including zero-day attacks. Using a baseline of typical behavior, unsupervised models are able to identify variations that may indicate security risks.

Techniques and Algorithms

Numerous unsupervised learning methods have been used to identify zero-day attacks:

- **Clustering Algorithms:** Similar data points are grouped using techniques like DBSCAN and K-means, enabling the identification of outliers that may represent anomalous behavior. These algorithms have been widely utilized in pattern recognition publications for intrusion detection systems.

- **Dimensionality Reduction:** Data complexity is decreased by methods like Principal Component Analysis (PCA), highlighting significant variations that could indicate anomalies.

- **Autoencoders:** Autoencoders, which use neural networks to learn effective coding of input data, may reconstruct data and use reconstruction mistakes to detect abnormalities.

- **Isolation Forests:** An algorithm that separates observations by first choosing a feature at random, and then choosing a split value at random from the feature's maximum and lowest values. The speed at which anomalies are separated makes this technique useful for intrusion detection.

Applications in Zero-Day Attack Detection

Unsupervised learning has been applied across various domains to detect zero-day attacks:

- **Network Intrusion Detection Systems (NIDS):** By analyzing network traffic, unsupervised models can identify unusual patterns indicative of potential intrusions. An extensive analysis of methods for detecting zero-day attacks based on machine learning highlights the effectiveness of these models in capturing statistical characteristics of attacks.

- **Web Application Security:** Unsupervised learning models monitor web traffic to detect anomalies that may signify assaults like cross-site scripting and SQL injection. The RETSINA framework, for instance, utilizes meta-learning to detect zero-day web attacks across different domains with limited training data.

- **Industrial Control Systems:** In critical infrastructure, unsupervised models analyze sensor data to identify deviations from normal operations, potentially indicating security breaches.

Challenges and Limitations

Despite their potential, unsupervised learning models face several challenges in zero-day attack detection:

- **High False Positive Rates:** Without labeled data, these models may flag benign anomalies as malicious, leading to false positives. Balancing sensitivity and specificity is crucial to minimize these occurrences.

- **Adaptability to Evolving Threats:** Unsupervised models must be able to adjust to new attack patterns in order to stay successful in the face of constantly changing cyber threats. Models that can manage the dynamic nature of zero-day assaults are essential, according to an assessment of unsupervised learning algorithms.

- **Computational Complexity:** Implementing unsupervised models in real-time systems requires effective algorithms that can quickly handle massive amounts of data.

- **Data Quality and Availability:** The quantity and quality of data have a significant impact on how well-unsupervised learning models perform. Insufficient or skewed data may result in subpar model performance.

Advancements and Future Directions

Recent research has focused on enhancing the capabilities of unsupervised learning in zero-day attack detection:

- **Hybrid Models:** Combining supervised and unsupervised learning approaches can yield more robust detection systems. A two-layer stacking model, for example, integrates both methods to effectively identify known and unknown threats.

- **Meta-Learning Approaches:** Leveraging knowledge from multiple domains enhances detection capabilities across various contexts. The RETSINA framework employs meta-learning to detect zero-day web attacks across different domains with limited training data, demonstrating improved performance over traditional methods.

- **Zero-Shot Learning:** This approach aims to detect attacks that were not existing in the training data by understanding the underlying attributes of known attacks and applying this knowledge to identify new, unseen threats. A study on zero-shot machine learning highlights its potential in zero-day attack detection.

3.7 Feature Selection and Model Optimization

The process of feature selection selects a subset of the original characteristics in order to minimize the feature space as much as possible based on a predetermined criterion.

A crucial phase in the feature creation process is feature selection. Some terms just don't show up very often in text categorization challenges. One training material may contain the phrase "groovy," which is a good thing. Is it truly worth maintaining this term as a feature? It's a risky endeavor since it's difficult to determine if a single training sample is indeed connected with the positive class or whether it's simply noise. It is possible that your learning system will be intelligent enough to solve it. Or you could simply take it off.

Three broad categories of feature selection algorithms exist: Methods for filters, wrappers, and embedding.

In machine learning, feature selection's function is,

To make the feature space less dimensional.

1. To accelerate an algorithm for learning.

2. To raise a classification algorithm's predicted accuracy.

3. To make the learning outcomes easier to understand.

The following are examples of feature selection algorithms:

1. **Instance-based approaches:** The process for creating feature subsets is not well defined. From the data, several little data samples are taken. For a data sample, features are weighted based on how well they distinguish instances of various classes. Higher-weighted features might be chosen.

2. **Nondeterministic approaches:** Feature selection also makes use of simulated annealing and genetic algorithms.

3. **Exhaustive complete approaches:** Branch and Bound assesses the estimated accuracy, whereas ABB verifies a monotonic inconsistency measure. Prior to the preset bound being unmaintainable, both begin with the whole feature set.

We encounter many characteristics in the dataset when developing a machine learning model for a real-world dataset, and not all of these features are always significant. When superfluous characteristics are included during model training, the model becomes biassed, loses its overall accuracy, becomes more complicated, and loses its capacity for generalization. The machine learning model is no exception to the adage "sometimes less is better." Therefore, one of the crucial stages in creating a machine-learning model is feature selection. Its objective is to identify the ideal feature set for creating a machine-learning model.

Several widely used feature selection methods in machine learning include:

- Filter methods
- Wrapper methods
- Embedded methods

Filter Methods

Set of all features → Selecting the best subset → Learning algorithm → Performance

Figure 4.1: Filter Methods Implementation

Source: - *(Geeksforgeeks, 2024)*

These techniques are often applied during the pre-processing phase. These techniques choose features from the dataset without utilizing any machine learning algorithms. These techniques are highly effective in eliminating redundant, correlated, and duplicated features, but they do not eliminate multicollinearity. They are also very quick and cheap to compute. Individual feature selection is assessed, which can occasionally be beneficial when features are independent of one another but will lag when a combination of characteristics might improve the model's overall performance.

Some techniques used are:

- **Information Gain:** It measures the decrease in entropy values and is defined as the quantity of information the feature offers for determining the goal value. Each attribute's information gain is computed taking into account the desired feature selection values.

- **Chi-square test:** A common technique for examining the association between categorical variables is the chi-square approach (X2). It contrasts the predicted value of the dataset with the observed values from various characteristics.

- **Fisher's Score:** A suboptimal collection of features is produced by Fisher's Score, which chooses each feature separately based on its scores under the Fisher criteria. The better the chosen attribute, the higher the Fisher's score.

- **Correlation Coefficient:** Pearson's Correlation Coefficient, which has values between -1 and 1, is a metric used to assess the link between two continuous variables and its direction.

- **Variance Threshold:** This strategy eliminates any features whose variance is less than a threshold. This technique automatically eliminates attributes with zero variance. This approach makes the assumption that traits with more variation would likely contain more information.

- **Mean Absolute Difference (MAD):** Although there is no square in MAD, this approach is comparable to the variance threshold method. The mean absolute difference from the mean value is computed using this approach.

- **Dispersion Ratio:** The ratio of the geometric mean (GM) to the arithmetic mean (AM) for a certain feature is known as the dispersion ratio. As $AM \geq GM$ for a certain characteristic, its value falls between +1 and ∞. A more significant characteristic is implied by a higher dispersion ratio.

- **Mutual Dependence:** This approach determines if two variables are mutually dependent and, if so, how much information can be gleaned about one variable by looking at the other. It calculates how much information a feature adds to the goal prediction based on whether it is present or absent.

- **Relief:** In order to determine the quality of attributes, this approach randomly selects one instance from the dataset, updates each feature, and separates nearby instances depending on how the selected instance differs from the two closest examples of the same and opposite classes.

Wrapper methods

Wrapper techniques, often known as greedy algorithms, use an iterative process to train the algorithm using a subset of characteristics. Feature addition and deletion occurs based on the results drawn by the model's pre-training training. The individual training the model typically pre-defines stopping conditions for choosing the best subset, such as when the model no longer performs as well or a certain number of characteristics are reached. Although they are more computationally costly, wrapper approaches have the primary benefit over filter methods in that they offer the best collection of data for model training, improving accuracy.

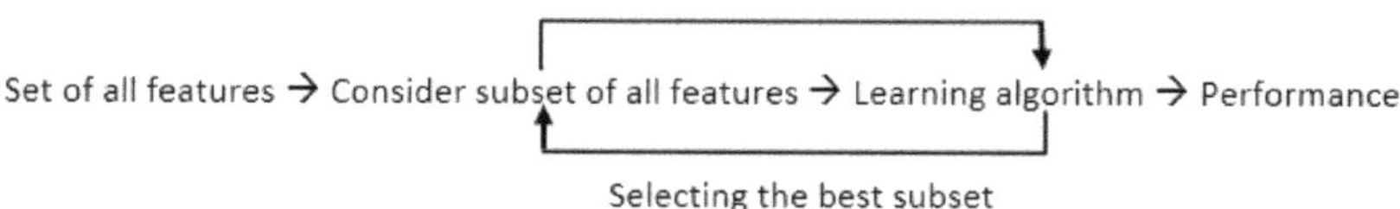

Figure 4.2: Wrapper Methods Implementation

Source: *- (Geeksforgeeks, 2024)*

Some techniques used are:

- **Forward selection:** A feature that best enhances our model is added after each iteration of this iterative process, which begins with an empty collection of features. Until adding a new variable does not enhance the model's performance, this is the stopping condition.

- **Backward elimination:** This technique is likewise iterative, starting with every feature and eliminating the least important one at the end of each iteration. The halting condition is until the feature is eliminated and no improvement in the model's performance is shown.

- **Bi-directional elimination:** This approach concurrently use the forward selection and backward elimination techniques to arrive at a single, distinct answer.

- **Exhaustive selection:** This method is regarded as the brute force approach to feature subset assessment. All potential subsets are generated, a learning algorithm is constructed for each subset, and the subset with the best model performance is chosen.

- **Recursive elimination:** In order to choose features, this greedy optimization technique repeatedly takes into account an ever-tinier collection of features. Feature_importance_attribute is used to determine the importance of the initial set of features that are used to train the estimator. Then, until the necessary number of features remain, the least significant characteristics are eliminated from the existing collection.

Embedded methods

Embedded techniques have their own built-in feature selection methods since the feature selection algorithm is integrated within the learning process. The disadvantages of filter and wrapper approaches are confronted by embedded techniques, which combine their benefits. These techniques are quicker than filter methods, more accurate than filter methods, and also take into account a variety of factors.

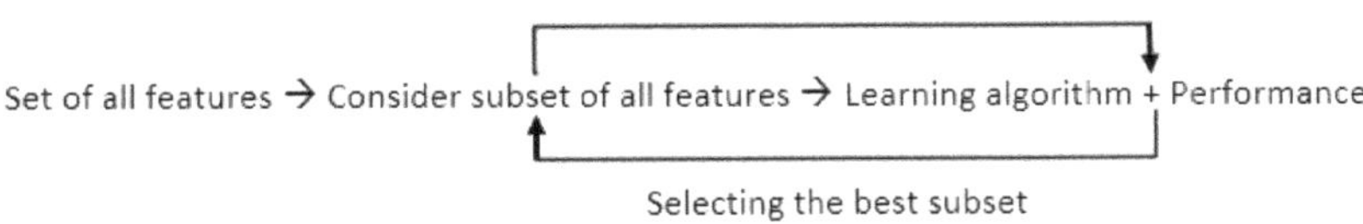

Figure 4.3: Embedded Methods Implementation

Source: - *(Geeksforgeeks, 2024)*

Some techniques used are:

- **Regularization:** To prevent the machine learning model from overfitting, this technique applies a penalty to certain model parameters. Elastic nets (L1 and L2 regularization) and Lasso (L1 regularization) are used in this feature selection method. Certain coefficients are reduced to zero by applying the penalty across the coefficients. It is possible to exclude features with zero coefficients from the dataset.

- **Tree-based methods:** These techniques, like Random Forest and Gradient Boosting, provide us feature significance as a means of feature selection. Feature importance identifies the features that have the greatest influence on the target feature.

3.8 Real-Time Detection Using ML and DL

Real-time detection powered by machine learning (ML) and deep learning (DL) represents a critical technological advancement that allows systems to analyze data streams instantaneously and respond to patterns or anomalies as they occur. This capability has revolutionized industries by enabling swift decision-making and enhancing operational efficiency. Applications range from network security and autonomous vehicles to healthcare monitoring and fraud prevention, making real-time detection an indispensable tool in modern systems.

Real-time detection systems consist of several integral components that work in harmony to deliver timely and accurate results. Data acquisition is the first step, where information is continuously gathered from sources such as IoT devices, sensors, or video streams. This data is then pre-processed to improve its quality and format, often involving techniques like noise reduction and normalization. Pre-processed data is analyzed by ML or DL models, which make predictions or classifications in real time. Finally, these predictions trigger immediate actions, such as sending alerts, activating safety measures, or logging information for further review.

Network security is one of the most important areas that uses real-time detection. Distributed Denial of Service (DDoS) attacks are one type of cyber threat, phishing attempts, and zero-day exploits can cause immense damage if not addressed immediately. AI-driven models analyze network traffic for unusual patterns, enabling organizations to identify and counter threats in real time. Similarly, in healthcare, wearable devices equipped with ML and DL models continuously monitor vital signs, detecting irregularities such as arrhythmias and alerting medical professionals promptly. This capability not only enhances patient care but can also save lives in critical situations.

Real-time object recognition and decision-making are critical in autonomous cars. Convolutional neural networks (CNNs) and other DL models are used by cars to identify things, pedestrians, and road signs, ensuring safe navigation even in dynamic environments. Fraud detection systems also benefit greatly from real-time detection by monitoring transactional data for anomalies that could indicate fraudulent activities. This proactive approach helps financial institutions minimize losses and maintain customer trust.

Machine learning techniques for real-time detection include reinforcement learning, supervised learning, and unsupervised learning. In order to train models for particular objectives, like spam identification or credit card fraud prevention, supervised learning uses labelled datasets. Conversely, unsupervised learning, is invaluable for detecting unknown anomalies or patterns, as it does not require labeled data. This approach is often employed in zero-day threat detection, where the system identifies new threats without prior knowledge. Because reinforcement learning enables models to learn from their interactions with the environment, detection systems are further improved over time.

In order to improve real-time detection, deep learning is essential. Applications like facial recognition, medical imaging, and autonomous driving are made possible by models like CNNs, which are crucial for processing visual input. Recurrent neural networks (RNNs) are useful for sentiment analysis and stock market forecasting because they are perfect for evaluating time-series data. Often employed in natural language processing (NLP), transformer-based models have also shown promise in video analytics. Hybrid models that combine ML and DL approaches offer even greater efficiency and accuracy, as seen in systems that integrate Random Forests with CNNs.

Real-time detection is fraught with difficulties, despite its revolutionary promise. One major obstacle is still achieving reduced latency while preserving good accuracy under various circumstances. Because of resource limitations, especially in devices with low processing power, model optimization using strategies like pruning and quantization is required. Furthermore, creative approaches are needed to guarantee scalability and resilience in large-scale implementations, such smart cities. Concerns about security and privacy also surface while handling sensitive real-time data, highlighting the necessity of strict security measures and adherence to privacy regulations.

These issues are still being addressed by technological advancements. By processing data closer to its source, edge computing, for instance, lowers latency and facilitates quicker decision-making. The viability of real-time detection on devices with limited resources is further improved by model optimization strategies like knowledge distillation and lightweight architectures. Scalability and low latency performance are balanced in hybrid systems that include Cloud and edge computing. Additionally, current research attempts to increase detection systems' resistance to hostile assaults and environmental changes, guaranteeing dependable performance in practical applications.

The significant influence of real-time detection is demonstrated through case examples. DL models are used by autonomous cars, such those with Tesla's Autopilot, to identify and react to road conditions in real time, allowing them to operate safely in challenging areas. Financial institutions use machine learning (ML)-based fraud prevention systems to keep an eye on transactions and stop illegal activity right away. Real-time health data are tracked by smart wearables using DL models in the healthcare industry, enabling prompt emergency treatments. Smart city projects use real-time data analytics powered by machine learning (ML) to optimize energy use, control traffic, and improve public safety.

Real-time detection has a bright future since quantum computing breakthroughs might completely transform its potential. Data processing speeds might increase exponentially with quantum computing, further reducing latency and enabling even more complex real-time detection tasks. Enhanced model interpretability will increase transparency, particularly in sensitive applications like healthcare and finance, fostering trust among users. Scalable IoT networks integrated with ML and DL will expand the reach and efficiency of real-time systems, enabling widespread adoption in industries such as logistics, transportation, and defense. Autonomous systems will continue to evolve, becoming smarter, faster, and more reliable, driving innovation across multiple sectors.

Real-time detection using ML and DL is reshaping industries by enabling instantaneous decision-making and improving efficiency. While challenges such as latency, accuracy, and resource constraints remain, advancements in technology are steadily overcoming these hurdles. As computational power and algorithmic sophistication continue to grow, real-time detection systems will unlock new possibilities, offering unparalleled accuracy, scalability, and adaptability. This technological evolution ensures a future where real-time detection becomes an integral part of daily operations across diverse applications.

3.9 Chapter Summary

The use of unsupervised learning in identifying zero-day attacks—which take use of unidentified flaws in systems—is examined in this chapter. Because conventional signature-based techniques are unable to identify these assaults, unsupervised learning must be used to spot irregularities in system behaviour and network traffic. The chapter discusses various unsupervised learning techniques, such as clustering algorithms (K-means, DBSCAN), dimensionality reduction (PCA), autoencoders, and isolation forests, which help detect previously unseen threats by establishing baselines of normal behavior. It highlights the role of unsupervised learning in network intrusion detection systems, web application security, and industrial control systems. However, challenges like high false positive rates, adaptability to evolving threats, computational complexity, and data quality limitations are also addressed. Advancements like hybrid models, meta-learning, and zero-shot learning are discussed as ways to improve detection capabilities. In order to maximize model performance, the chapter also discusses feature selection strategies, such as filter, wrapper, and embedding approaches. Machine learning and deep learning-powered real-time detection systems are crucial for ongoing data analysis and threat response. The chapter ends by stressing how crucial it is to combine real-time detection models with unsupervised learning in order to protect dynamic settings from emerging cyber threats.

Multiple-choice questions (MCQs)

1. **What is the primary purpose of threat detection mechanisms in security systems?**

    a. To identify potential weaknesses in the system

    b. To monitor hardware performance

    c. To identify and respond to malicious activities or anomalies in a system

    d. To store sensitive data securely

2. **Which of the following is a common technique used to detect anomalies in cloud databases?**

    a. Linear regression

    b. Anomaly detection algorithms such as clustering or statistical methods

    c. Database replication

    d. Data compression techniques

3. **What is the role of classification algorithms in threat identification?**

   a. To separate data into categories and identify patterns that represent potential threats

   b. To encrypt sensitive data

   c. To optimize database performance

   d. To store threat data securely

4. **How can Natural Language Processing (NLP) be used in threat detection?**

   a. By processing and analyzing text data to identify suspicious content such as phishing attacks or malicious commands

   b. By performing hardware optimizations

   c. By encrypting data in cloud storage

   d. By managing network bandwidth

5. **What is the advantage of using unsupervised learning for zero-day attack detection?**

   a. It requires a lot of labeled data to train the model

   b. It can identify previously unseen attacks by detecting patterns in data without prior knowledge of specific threats

   c. It is faster than supervised learning techniques

   d. It is focused on enhancing system hardware

6. **What is the purpose of feature selection in machine learning models?**

   a. To reduce the computational cost of training models by selecting the most relevant features

   b. To increase the amount of data used for training

   c. To store models in cloud systems

   d. To optimize the speed of data transfer

7. **How does model optimization improve machine learning and deep learning models in threat detection?**

   a. By adjusting the model's parameters to improve performance and reduce errors

   b. By making the model compatible with multiple hardware configurations

   c. By reducing the model's storage size

   d. By increasing the size of the training dataset

8. **Which of the following is a key characteristic of real-time detection using machine learning and deep learning?**

   a. Models analyze data at a faster rate to detect and respond to threats in near real-time

   b. It requires extensive data pre-processing before analysis

   c. Models only detect threats after a system breach occurs

   d. It is used primarily for optimizing database performance

9. **What is the challenge of detecting zero-day attacks using machine learning?**

   a. There are too many features to choose from

   b. These attacks have no prior examples, making them hard to detect without historical data

   c. The attacks occur after the model is trained

   d. Zero-day attacks are easy to identify with traditional methods

10. **What type of data is primarily used in Natural Language Processing (NLP) for threat detection?**

    a. Numerical data

    b. Audio files

    c. Text data from sources like emails, logs, and websites

    d. Image data from network cameras

Answers

1	2	3	4	5	6	7	8	9	10
C	B	A	A	B	A	A	A	B	C

Chapter 04

PREVENTING THREATS USING AI-DRIVEN SECURITY MECHANISMS

4.1 Chapter Overview

This week's chapter discusses how cybersecurity can be improved using advanced ML and AI techniques. Starting with threat prevention, it deprecates perimeter strategies and includes ideas such as Next-Generation Firewalls (NGFWs), and mobile security. The flexibility, automation, and ability of machine learning to scale up are also explained, therefore directly managing on its promises for change based on shortcomings such as data problems and adversarial attack.

CNNs, RNNs, and GANs come into the frontline focus together with other deep learning methods in predictive analytics as well as database access control. These techniques enable organizations to prevent various and sophisticated cyber threats. Technological advances also transform patch management since AI discovers and tests the patches while deploying a secure system.

Another is data exfiltration prevention, which addresses the issue using training, identity management as well as online real-time monitoring. Detection and Response (EDR) and Intrusion Detection Systems (IDS) are two more cutting-edge technologies that boost proactive security. The chapter closes by noting an emerging dual cooperation between AI and human considerations with skills in thinking where computers offer adequacy and emphasis in fight against modern cyber threats.

4.2 Understanding the Importance of Threat Prevention

In network security, threat prevention refers to the procedures and equipment that safeguard your company network.

Threat prevention used to be mostly concerned with the perimeter. An integrated, multilayered approach to security is necessary for advanced threat prevention since a growing number of threats, including malware and ransomware, are being sent through phishing and spam emails. Tools for advanced malware protection, endpoint security threat prevention, and intrusion threat detection and prevention may be included in this.

Four steps for threat prevention

It might be quite difficult to provide adequate threat prevention. We provide five easy measures for preventing cyber threats in our network security checklist. We list the key elements below.

- **Secure the perimeter**

  The perimeter should be taken into account first. Antivirus software and traditional firewalls are no longer enough. However, to offer a multilayered approach, next-generation firewalls (NGFWs) include URL filtering, Application Visibility and Control (AVC), Next-Generation Intrusion Prevention System (NGIPS), and Advanced Malware Protection (AMP).

  To secure the perimeter and implement an integrated solution, an NGFW is an essential first step.

- **Protect users wherever they work**

  Currently, more than half of workers are mobile. IT needs to shift with the way workers work. The goal of IT security solutions should be to safeguard workers wherever they are employed. Workers may work from any place using a mobile device, including the main office and branch offices.

  Mobile device security has been the largest problem for the majority of IT teams. Businesses will continue to utilize more mobile devices; thus it is crucial to handle mobile device security even if it is challenging. Mobile device security may be instantly enhanced by technologies like virtual private networks (VPNs), user verification, and device trust.

- **Smart network segmentation**

  Your network is divided by software-defined segmentation, which makes it simple to isolate threats. Codependences can be challenging to spot as business apps and users grow. Businesses need sophisticated network security analytics and visibility to recognize all of a network's interdependencies in order to avoid threats effectively.

  Excessive network segmentation might cause lag. Attacks may spread if segments are not sufficiently separated. When segmenting, businesses need to be astute and effective.

- **Find and control problems fast**

  Security lapses will occur. Finding and eliminating issues is a key component of threat prevention. This calls for a great deal of visibility and control. IT workers who are prepared are also necessary. In order to be ready, we frequently advise companies to create an incident response strategy and use penetration testing to evaluate their present network solutions.

Types of threat prevention and detection solutions

- **NGFW**

  An NGFW is an essential initial step in threat prevention, as was previously discussed. Conventional firewalls just allow or prohibit access. Although this makes sense, its effectiveness depends on how well the rules and limitations have been implemented. For instance, IT is unlikely to have established procedures to prevent access to a danger if it is unknown and new.

  On the other hand, NGFWs interface with other software programs like AMP and NGIPS. These extra solutions offer capabilities for detection and mitigation to safeguard your network in the event that an unexpected danger eludes automatically implemented regulations. An NGFW gives you more visibility, automation, and control over your network with all of these additional tools.

- **NGIPS**

  Superior threat protection is offered by NGIPS in the areas of vulnerability and patch management, public Cloud, internal network segmentation, and intrusion detection.

  Technology for intrusion detection must adapt to changing threats. Consistent protection and insights about people, apps, devices, and network vulnerabilities are offered by NGIPS. NGIPS can swiftly identify threats by using integrated sandboxing and file-based inspection. NGIPS offers retroactive analysis to eliminate and correct threats late in their lifecycle if they manage to elude defenses.

  Enterprise organizations can offer a uniform enforcement system that covers the needs of various internal organizations by segmenting their networks. Different workloads and network needs may be easily accommodated via segmentation.

  NGIPS offers reliable security that is applied to both private and public Clouds. Multiple hypervisors, such as Azure, AWS, and

VMware, should be supported by your NGIPS. The virtual switches beneath do not affect these apps. Through deep packet inspection between containerized environments, NGIPS enables policy enforcement across the network on-premise devices, public Cloud infrastructure, and shared hypervisors.

Based on NGIPS findings, you may be more discriminating when it comes to vulnerabilities and patch management. Patching high priority vulnerabilities can frequently be delayed by an organization's test environment and/or methodology. Reduce the time and resources needed to implement these changes. It is much simpler to modify the IPS settings and never have to roll back a patch.

- **AMP**

  One essential element of next-generation systems is advanced malware protection. Malware keeps changing and adapting. Because of this, malware may be very challenging to find at the network's edge. Networks may find a lot more malware threats that were previously undiscovered by combining an NGFW with an AMP and threat intelligence.

  Even while threat intelligence can detect more risks, new, unheard-of malware will still pose a hazard to your network. Timer features and other covert features may be included in some of this malware, which masks harmful activity until it has infiltrated the network. However, certain AMP systems analyze files continually over the course of their lifetime. This is really important. With these features, AMP will promptly identify malware that later starts acting maliciously.

- **AVC**

  More applications than ever before are being used by businesses. A real application-aware network may be established by organizations using Application Visibility and Control (AVC) technologies. AVC may provide visibility and control over network applications by combining statistical categorization, socket caching, service discovery, auto-learning, DNS-AS, and deep packet inspection (DPI), which can categorize applications.

Increased visibility allows organizations to respond to threats much more quickly. Applications can occasionally constitute a network vulnerability. An organization cannot defend its apps if it is unable to view all of them. Monitoring and analytics for applications provide real-time information on their performance. Poor performance may indicate that there are dangers.

Threat intelligence

All of these solutions are strengthened by threat intelligence. Excellent threat intelligence elevates these technologies to the next level. An organization's capacity to thwart attacks is enhanced by network visibility and protection. However, all of this is predicated on an organization's ability to identify whether a file is safe or malicious. This is not likely. The network is unaware of the majority of threats.

If an unknown threat has been identified as harmful somewhere in the world, threat intelligence can notify your network. With threat intelligence, a large number of previously unknown risks are now fully recognized and comprehended!

User verification and device trust

Controlling network access is essential to security. Networks may enforce application access controls and build confidence with user identities and devices by using user verification and device trust solutions. Before granting users access to company data and resources, two-factor authentication can confirm their identity. Device trust solutions can examine devices during access to ascertain their security posture and reliability in addition to user verification.

4.3 Role of Machine Learning in Preventing Database Attacks

Cybersecurity threats are more prevalent than ever in today's constantly evolving digital landscape. Injection attacks, particularly SQL and NoSQL injections, are among the most dangerous vulnerabilities exploited by malicious actors. Injection attacks continue to rank among the top 10 most serious security threats, according to the Open Web Application Security Project (OWASP). According to Verizon's Data Breach Investigations Report from 2023, injection attacks were engaged in more than 30% of breaches, and according to Gartner, insufficient vulnerability management would be the cause of 80% of application security failures by 2025. Adopting cutting-edge methods to identify and stop these threats is essential given the constantly increasing sophistication of assaults, and machine learning (ML) is a key component in this process.

Understanding Injection Attacks: The Persistent Threat

Injection attacks involve injecting malicious code into a vulnerable system to manipulate the execution of its commands. These attacks often target databases, causing severe consequences like unauthorized data access, loss of data integrity, and system compromise. SQL injections, a common form of this threat, can result in massive data breaches and financial losses for businesses. According to the Ponemon Institute, SQL injection attacks were largely to blame for the average data breach cost of $4.45 million in 2023.

Traditional security measures, though effective to some extent, struggle to keep up with the sophisticated nature of modern injection attacks. Conventional rule-based security systems often fail to detect new and complex attack patterns, making businesses vulnerable to zero-day exploits. This is where machine learning can offer a game-changing solution.

The Power of Machine Learning in Security Testing

Machine learning has become a vital tool in the toolbox of cybersecurity professionals due to its capacity to analyze vast datasets and spot trends. In security testing, machine learning algorithms may be trained to identify irregularities, anticipate possible weaknesses, and adjust to new attack techniques, particularly injection assaults.

QualiZeal's AI/ML Injection Detector and Preventor technology ensures that user input is never blindly trusted and is always validated for its authenticity. This solution restricts, controls, and monitors all forms of user input, proactively detecting and preventing injection-based attacks. By leveraging AI/ML technologies, businesses can significantly mitigate risks like data loss, security breaches, and denial of service, thereby maintaining the integrity of their digital infrastructure.

Injection Attack Detection with ML Algorithms

The most promising ML models for detecting injection attacks are anomaly detection algorithms. These models learn what constitutes "normal" behavior for a given application. When a user input or query deviates from the norm, the ML system flags it as a potential threat. In these situations, algorithms such as Random Forest, Support Vector Machines (SVM), and Neural Networks are commonly employed because of their high accuracy in identifying questionable activity.

Advanced methods such as Natural Language Processing (NLP) models allow systems to examine user input and SQL queries to detect malicious payloads. NLP-based models greatly reduce false positives and false negatives by rapidly differentiating between benign and dangerous orders by comprehending the structure and content of inputs.

Malicious inputs including SQL, XSS, HTML, and command injection are prevented during the validation phase of QualiZeal's AI/ML-based injection detection solution. The system ensures real-time risk mitigation by creating logs and preventing such inputs from reaching crucial databases. (Qualizeal, 2024)

Benefits of ML-Enabled Injection Attack Detection and Prevention

Adopting machine learning for injection attack detection and prevention offers numerous advantages:

- **Improved Detection Accuracy:** ML models detect attacks with greater accuracy by learning from data, reducing false positives and negatives. QualiZeal's AI/ML Injection Detector ensures that malicious inputs are blocked early in the process.

- **Real-time Threat Mitigation:** With continuous monitoring and analysis, ML-powered systems identify injection attacks in real-time, enabling faster response. QualiZeal's solution generates logs and alerts in case of any injection attempt.

- **Adaptability to Emerging Threats:** ML models evolve as they are exposed to new threats, providing robust protection against future vulnerabilities.

- **Automation of Security Tasks:** Security teams may save time and money by automating repetitive testing procedures so they can concentrate on strategic projects. The AI/ML solutions from QualiZeal help automate the detection, recording, and prevention of injection assaults.

- **Scalability:** ML systems are perfect for companies of all kinds, from startups to large corporations, since they can manage enormous volumes of data.

Challenges in Implementing ML for Security Testing

Implementing machine learning (ML) for injection attack detection and prevention presents difficulties despite its potential. The quality of the data is one of the main obstacles. For ML models to work well, a lot of high-quality data is needed. Biassed or inaccurate data may result in missed assaults or, worse, false positives. Additionally, companies need to invest in qualified experts that are knowledgeable in both cybersecurity and machine learning due to the complexity of setting up and maintaining ML systems.

Another challenge is the potential for attackers to use adversarial techniques to trick ML models. By crafting inputs that exploit weaknesses in the ML system, attackers can bypass detection. To counter this, continuous model updates and adversarial testing are necessary to keep ML models robust.

- **Preventing Data Poisoning in AI**

  In spite of numerous benefits AI/ML technologies offer to business, cyber criminals now turn to AI/ML to launch attacks themselves. Data poisoning is growing more virulent than traditional attacks and is a critical issue for cyber security experts. Attackers attempt to incorporate the inputs into training data in this case, which compromises the system's capacity to provide precise predictions. Attackers will intentionally insert malicious material into training data for an ML system in order to change the system's behaviour or provide erroneous results.

To prevent data poisoning in AI, organizations can consider below points:

- **Ensure Data Integrity:** Establishing data governance and ensuring that the data used to train machine learning models is reliable and unaffected by malicious assaults are crucial. Access restrictions, encryption, and other security measures may be used in this situation.

- **Data Validation:** Prior to the data being included into the AI system, it is imperative that the data be verified for quality, accuracy, and consistency.

- **Monitor Data Inputs:** Carefully monitoring data inputs is essential to identifying and averting data poisoning attempts. This entails keeping an eye on the data's origin, the kinds of data being used, and any odd trends or patterns.

- **Data Filtering:** Malicious data may be kept out of the AI model by filtering the data before it enters the system. This entails eliminating information that doesn't adhere to quality criteria.

- **Data Diversification:** A diversified range of data can help prevent data poisoning. A range of data sets should be used to train the AI model in order to reduce the likelihood that an attacker may change a specific dataset.

- **Implement Outlier Detection:** Finding and flagging any data points that deviate considerably from the norm can be aided by outlier detection. This might be used to stop harmful data from entering the system.

- **Conduct Regular Security Audits:** The machine learning system's vulnerabilities and flaws can be found with the use of routine security audits. This can enhance security overall and help stop data poisoning attempts.

- **Access Control:** To limit access to the data required to train the AI model, access control measures should be implemented.

- **Robust Models:** Data poisoning may be avoided by developing a strong AI model. A strong model is able to recognize and disregard harmful data or adjust to data changes.

- **Frequent Label Checks:** It is important for scientists creating AI models to regularly verify the accuracy of the labels used in the training data.

- **Open Source Data Usage:** Although using open source data facilitates the creation of accurate models, attackers will find these models to be a profitable target.

- **Penetration Testing:** Vulnerabilities that provide outsiders access to data training models can be discovered via penetration testing and offensive security testing.

- **Additional Layer of AI/ML:** Another option is to create a second layer of AI and ML to detect any mistakes in data training.

- **Awareness of Employees:** Attackers frequently use employees' ignorance to gain access to an organization. Workers must get training on how to avoid common social engineering scams like phishing.

Data Poisoning is a major area of concern. Proper planning should be put in place to prevent attacks as much as possible.

4.4 Predictive Analytics for Threat Mitigation

The gathering, evaluating, and sharing of data on possible or existing risks to an organization's digital assets is known as cyber threat intelligence or CTI. It encompasses data about threats from various sources, including malware, vulnerabilities, attack vectors, and threat actors.

CTI seeks to offer useful information that businesses may utilize to improve their security posture and successfully counteract online attacks. Cyber Threat Intelligence (CTI) is not only about gathering data but also involves the contextual analysis of that data to derive actionable insights. This process includes understanding the motivations behind cyber-attacks, the capabilities of threat actors, and the specific vulnerabilities that may be exploited in an organization's infrastructure.

CTI operates on several key principles:

1. **Contextualization:** Threat intelligence goes beyond raw data to provide context. This includes understanding the significance of a threat in relation to an organization's specific environment, the potential impact on critical assets, and how it aligns with business objectives.

2. **Timeliness:** In the fast-paced world of cyber threats, timely information is crucial. CTI must provide up-to-date intelligence that reflects the latest threat landscape, allowing organizations to respond rapidly to emerging threats.

3. **Actionability:** Effective CTI translates complex threat data into actionable recommendations. This involves providing specific guidance on how to mitigate risks or respond to particular threats, enabling organizations to take informed defensive measures.

4. **Integration:** CTI should be integrated into the broader security operations of an organization. This integration ensures that threat intelligence informs security policies, incident response plans, and risk management strategies.

5. **Collaboration:** The sharing of threat intelligence across organizations and sectors enhances collective security. Working together can increase overall resistance against cyberattacks and result in a more thorough knowledge of risks.

CTI can be categorized into three main types:

1. **Strategic Threat Intelligence:** This type focuses on high-level insights for decision-makers, covering trends, motivations, and capabilities of threat actors. It influences long-term security policies and resource allocation.

2. **Operational Threat Intelligence:** This provides details about specific threats, such as the attackers' tactics, methods, and procedures (TTPs) and indications of compromise (IOCs). Implementing protective measures is crucial for security teams.

3. **Tactical Threat Intelligence:** This type includes technical details relevant for immediate operational responses, such as filtering out malicious network traffic, detecting malware, or responding to specific incidents.

Importance of Predictive Analytics in Cybersecurity

Predictive analytics is essential for improving CTI because it enables businesses to foresee and stop possible cyber threats before they become real. Unlike traditional reactive approaches that focus on responding to incidents after they occur, predictive analytics leverages historical data and machine learning algorithms to spot trends, patterns, and irregularities that might point to potential assaults in the future.

Key benefits of predictive analytics in cyber security include:

1. **Proactive Threat Detection:** Predictive analytics helps organizations anticipate possible attacks and make appropriate preparations by examining historical events and present danger landscapes. This proactive stance reduces the likelihood of successful breaches.

2. **Improved Resource Allocation:** Based on anticipated risks, organizations may prioritize their security activities, guaranteeing efficient resource allocation. The effectiveness of security operations is increased by this focused strategy.

3. **Enhanced Incident Response:** Predictive models can provide security teams with insights into potential attack methods and the expected impact, allowing for quicker and more informed incident response.

4. **Risk Management:** Predictive analytics aids in assessing the risk levels associated with various threats, facilitating informed decision-making and prioritization of security measures based on risk exposure.

5. **Continuous Improvement:** Organizations may improve their threat detection skills and adjust to the constantly changing cyber threat landscape by regularly adding fresh data to prediction models.

The Role of Predictive Analytics in Cyber Threat Intelligence

In the subject of Cyber Threat Intelligence (CTI), predictive analytics is essential since it changes how businesses handle cyber security. Utilizing past data and sophisticated analytical methods, predictive analytics improves threat detection capabilities and permits preventative actions against possible intrusions. This section explores the various ways predictive analytics contributes to effective cyber threat management.

A. Enhancing Threat Detection Capabilities

1. **Identifying Patterns and Trends**

    The capacity of predictive analytics in CTI to spot patterns and trends in cyber threat data is one of its main purposes. Through the analysis of historical incidents, organizations can uncover recurring behaviours and tactics used by threat actors. This capability is essential for several reasons:

    - **Behavioral Analysis:** Predictive analytics enables security teams to study past attack patterns, revealing how different types of cyber-attacks evolve over time. For instance, analyzing the frequency and nature of phishing attempts can help identify common characteristics that are prevalent in specific industries or against certain organizations.

    - **Anomaly Detection:** Predictive analytics may identify departures from the norm and indicate possible hazards by creating a baseline of typical network behavior. By continually learning from fresh data, machine learning algorithms might improve their capacity to identify abnormalities that can point to criminal activity.

    - **Trend Forecasting:** Based on past data, predictive models can identify patterns, assisting organizations in being ready for potential attack points.

For instance, companies can put preventative measures in place to protect against a certain virus kind if it is shown to be becoming more common. Finding patterns and trends helps with both short-term threat identification and long-term security strategy development.

2. **Real-time Analysis of Threat Data**

The capacity for real-time analysis is another significant aspect of predictive analytics in CTI. As cyber threats evolve rapidly, organizations must be able to respond instantly to emerging risks. Predictive analytics facilitates real-time data processing through:

- **Automated Threat Detection:** By using predictive models that analyze live data streams, organizations can detect threats as they occur. Machine learning algorithms, for instance, are able to evaluate incoming network traffic in real time and spot possible attack indicators such anomalous traffic spikes or illegal access attempts.

- **Continuous Monitoring:** Predictive analytics allows for ongoing surveillance of an organization's digital environment. By consistently examining information from several sources, including logs and intrusion detection systems, security teams can receive immediate alerts when suspicious activities are detected.

- **Incident Response Activation:** Real-time analysis enables organizations to activate incident response plans more swiftly. Automated solutions can minimize the possible effect of an attack by launching pre-programmed actions, including blocking malicious IP addresses or isolating compromised computers, as soon as a potential danger is detected. By combining automated detection with real-time analysis, organizations may maintain a proactive security posture and lower the chance of successful attacks.

B. Anticipating Future Threats

Beyond enhancing detection capabilities, Predictive analytics enables businesses to foresee potential risks and take preventative measures. This element is crucial in a world where cyber threats are ever-changing.

1. **Predicting Attack Vectors**

    Predictive analytics provides valuable insights into potential attack vectors, helping organizations prepare for future threats. This predictive capability involves:

    - **Threat Actor Profiling:** Through the examination of known threat actors' tactics, methods, and procedures (TTPs), predictive analytics can pinpoint probable future actions. For instance, if a specific group is known for exploiting a certain vulnerability, organizations can prioritize defense against that vector.

    - **Environmental Scanning:** Predictive models can assess changes in the cyber threat landscape, including newly discovered vulnerabilities, emerging malware strains, and shifts in attack trends. By understanding these dynamics, organizations can adapt their security measures accordingly.

    - **Scenario Planning:** Predictive analytics enables organizations to simulate various threat scenarios based on historical data and current trends. This modeling helps security teams Determine the possible effects of various assault methods and create tactical countermeasures. Anticipating attack vectors helps organizations strengthen their defenses and lower the likelihood of successful breaches.

2. **Risk Assessment and Prioritization**

    In order to focus on the most urgent dangers and allocate resources effectively, organizations must practice effective risk management. Prioritization and risk assessment are improved by predictive analytics through:

- **Quantitative Risk Assessment:** Predictive models allow organizations to precisely evaluate their risk exposure by quantifying the likelihood and possible effect of different threats. By integrating threat intelligence data with organizational context, predictive analytics provides a clearer picture of vulnerabilities.

- **Prioritizing Security Initiatives:** Based on the risk assessments generated by predictive analytics, organizations can prioritize their security initiatives. This prioritization ensures that resources are allocated to address the most significant threats, maximizing the effectiveness of security investments.

- **Continuous Risk Monitoring:** Predictive analytics supports continuous risk assessment by constantly updating models with new data. This ongoing evaluation allows organizations to adapt their risk management strategies in real-time, responding to emerging threats proactively.

By facilitating comprehensive risk assessment and prioritization, predictive analytics empowers organizations to allocate resources and decide on their security posture with knowledge.

Predictive analytics plays a pivotal role in enhancing cyber threat intelligence by improving threat detection capabilities and enabling organizations to anticipate future threats. Through the identification of patterns and trends, Realtime analysis of threat data, and proactive risk assessment, organizations can strengthen their defense against evolving cyber threats. As the cyber landscape continues to change, the integration of predictive analytics into cyber security strategies will be essential for maintaining resilience and safeguarding digital assets.

4.5 AI Powered Threat Intelligence Sharing

The Transformative Impact of AI on Threat Intelligence and Cyber Defence

The area of threat intelligence has undergone a major transformation as a result of AI, becoming faster and more effective at catching and responding to cyber threats. Using machine learning and natural language processing (NLP), AI mitigates the volume of cyber threat data analysts are confronted with, improving the accuracy and relevance of threat detection, while reducing false positives. Nearly every phase of the threat intelligence lifecycle is optimized by AI. It automates data gathering from scattered sources such as dark web, social media and open source intelligence in planning and collection phase. It uses keyword and pattern recognition to filter out the relevant data and uses NLP to interpret unstructured text to derive the actionable insights. During processing and analysis AI cleans up redundancies, finds anomalies, and correlates IP addresses and email addresses with known threats, enriching data context (and correlation). AI is applied at the production stage, turning intelligence into comprehensive reports with visual aids such as charts and heat maps to make intelligence available to decision makers. Two types of feedback loops do the remaining things to improve AI models, and they help refine the threat detection and mitigation.

Real time monitoring and analysis of abnormalities and potential threats is what Ai based threat protection is. Automated threat responses make response time short, and reduce human error by patching vulnerabilities or isolating compromised systems. Incorporated threat data from across the spectrum of security scenarios is integrated by AI, enabling better decision making. AI's use cases for threat intelligence go beyond imagination. The data it brings in from different platforms, patterns, indicators of compromise (IoCs), and monitors the dark web for sensitive data and provides contextual threat analysis based on organization's risks. Predictive capabilities are also improved thanks to AI, from identifying new threats and attack vectors to preventively defending.

But AI is scalable, efficient and more accurate. AI systems are vulnerable to adversarial attacks, and one probably cannot depend too much on AI, at least in creating integrated models of essential services. Its implementation is complicated by bias in the algorithms, and regulatory compliance. To move the future of AI in threat intelligence forward, we must continue to increase predictive analytics, improve NLP for greater accuracy, and encourage human-AI cooperation, to navigate complex security environments. AI and human expertise will build a robust cyber defense against evolving cyber threats together.

Which parts of the intelligence cycle can be powered by AI, how and why?

Nearly every phase of the threat intelligence lifecycle, a methodical structure that aids businesses in producing, managing, and efficiently using threat intelligence, may be improved by AI.

- **Planning and collection**

  AI can automate and speed up the data-collecting process throughout the threat intelligence lifecycle's collection phase. It can search through enormous volumes of data from a variety of sources, such as reports, social media, dark web forums, and open-source intelligence, to find pertinent information. AI can filter out pertinent data by identifying certain keywords, patterns, and indicators of compromise (IoCs) in the gathered data through the use of keyword and pattern recognition. AI can interpret human language and derive valuable threat intelligence from unstructured text sources, such news stories and blogs, thanks to Natural Language Processing (NLP).

- **Processing and analysis**

  AI algorithms may identify and eliminate redundant or duplicate items in gathered data throughout the processing and analysis phase of the lifecycle. This makes it possible for the system to identify irregularities in the data and eliminate unnecessary information. AI is able to identify entities in the data, including email addresses, domain names, and IP addresses, and correlate them with threat actors or known threats. Additionally, it can recognize important details, emotions, and context to help make data easier to comprehend and use.

- **Production and dissemination**

  AI can automatically create threat intelligence reports at the production and distribution stages of the threat intelligence lifecycle by compiling, condensing, and arranging pertinent data into reports that are clear, actionable, and accessible by humans. To aid analysts and decision-makers in comprehending intricate threat trends and linkages, these reports may incorporate visual representations of threat data, such as heatmaps, charts, and graphs. By translating threat intelligence into several languages for a worldwide audience, AI can even make multilingual threat reporting easier.

- **Feedback and improvement**

  AI's training process is guided by its feedback loop throughout the threat intelligence lifecycle's feedback stage, which enables AI to gradually develop and enhance its threat identification and intelligence-gathering skills.

  AI may modify its algorithms and procedures to give more pertinent threat information by taking stakeholder concerns and requirements into account. This helps businesses better detect and address the dangers at hand.

This helps businesses to concentrate their efforts to guard against the most pertinent and urgent security concerns, continually improve their threat detection skills, and stay up to date with changing threat environments.

What is AI based threat protection?

AI-based threat protection, as used in threat intelligence, is the process of continually monitoring for and identifying possible risks to an organization using artificial intelligence, including machine learning algorithms.

Real-time processing and analysis of massive volumes of data by AI technology allows it to accurately identify abnormalities and possible dangers. In order to provide organizations with the actionable insight they require to proactively and successfully manage security risks, artificial intelligence (AI) can extract relevant data about possible threats.

- **Automated threat response and decision-making**

Based on the intelligence acquired, AI may automate threat responses to known or specified dangers in incident response. This may entail patching, banning malicious IP addresses, or isolating affected systems. The window of vulnerability can be decreased by using automated reactions, which can be carried out more quickly than manual intervention.

By incorporating threat information feeds, AI can support decision-making and help businesses remain abreast of emerging risks and attack methods. This integration guarantees that the most up-to-date threat data is used to inform choices and responses.

A more thorough understanding of a security issue may also be obtained by using AI to correlate data from a variety of sources. In order to detect risks and support decision-making and reaction tactics, it can connect apparently unconnected cyber, geopolitical, and physical security events.

In order to help security teams, prioritize their actions and advise decision-makers on the best ways to reduce risk, artificial intelligence (AI) may also help create intelligence on the likelihood, severity, and possible effect of attacks. This guarantees that the most important threats are dealt with first, cutting down on reaction times and limiting harm.

Use cases of AI in threat intelligence

From data collection and processing to analysis and reporting, artificial intelligence has several applications in threat intelligence.

Specifically, this includes:

- **Aggregating threat data** – providing a thorough picture of possible threats by gathering and combining information from a variety of sources, such as the deep and dark web, open-source, external threat feeds, and reports.

- **Natural Language Processing (NLP)** – From textual threat data, pertinent information is extracted and threat intelligence data is enhanced.

- **Pattern recognition** – Finding trends and irregularities in threat data to assist threat intelligence analysts in identifying new attack avenues and weaknesses

- **Discovering IOCs** – Simplify the IOC extraction process by locating IOCs in threat data, such as dubious IP addresses, domains, or file hashes.

- **Tactics, Techniques and Procedures (TTPs)** –To better defend against certain adversary behaviours and identify the threat individuals or groups responsible for particular assaults, past attack patterns, tactics, strategies, and processes are analyzed.

Dark web monitoring – Finding references to a company's data, passwords, or other private information on the dark web in order to provide early warnings of possible breaches

- **Contextual threat analysis** – Analysing threat data in the context of an organization's industry, geography, and priorities, providing a more tailored assessment of potential risk

- **Threat classification** –Threats are automatically categorized and prioritized according to their importance and seriousness.

- **Threat intelligence Reporting** – Creating threat intelligence reports that facilitate leadership and security teams' comprehension of the current threat landscape and decision-making

Advantages and Risks of AI in Threat Intelligence

Although AI threat intelligence has many advantages, there are hazards and difficulties involved as well.

Advantages of AI

- **Enhanced speed and efficiency** – Real-time processing and analysis of massive volumes of data using AI technology boosts output and facilitates quicker threat identification and reaction.

- **Improved accuracy** – AI can detect and extract information that people would overlook, lowering the possibility of human error from supervision, data input mistakes, and other human variables. This results in more accurate threat assessments.

- **Continuous monitoring** – Because AI systems are fatigue-free, they can operate around the clock, maintaining alertness and facilitating prompt reactions to new dangers.

- **Predictive capabilities** – Based on past data, AI and machine learning algorithms can spot patterns and forecast potential dangers, improving decision-making and assisting companies in proactively defending against changing attack vectors.

- **Scalability** – AI is capable of handling shifting data and alert quantities, carrying out intricate activities, and successfully and economically adjusting to changing demands.

Risks and challenges of AI

- **Adversarial attacks** – The efficacy of AI-based threat intelligence can be undermined by skilled threat actors who try to trick AI systems by creating assaults that are intentionally made to avoid detection.

- **Balancing human-AI collaboration** – It might be difficult to find the ideal balance between AI systems and human analysts. In order to properly assess dangers, human specialists still need to contribute critical thinking, creativity, context, and ethical judgment, even though AI can offer important insights. An over-reliance on AI may result in mistakes and hazards being overlooked.

- **Bias concerns** – Biases in training data or algorithms can be absorbed and reinforced by AI models, leading to inaccurate or misleading evaluations.

- **Regulatory compliance** – Organisations using AI in threat intelligence may need to negotiate intricate and changing regulatory frameworks, which may be expensive and time-consuming.

The future of AI in threat intelligence

The capabilities and applications of AI in threat intelligence will only increase because of its innate capacity for learning and development.

This might involve advancements in predictive analytics and AI's capacity to evaluate more complex and dynamic dangers, such as advanced persistent threats (APTs) and zero-day assaults. AI-powered natural language processing (NLP) tools might improve multilingualism and more accurately identify and assess moods and emotions in text.

To analyze and offer a contextual understanding of AI-driven threat intelligence, human skills will still be crucial. In order to make decisions and reduce risk, humans must be able to evaluate hazards using critical thinking as well as ethical, legal, and practical concerns. Threat intelligence frequently covers complex, multidimensional scenarios, and even with AI's advances, human judgement, and flexibility are still necessary.

4.6 Preventing Data Exfiltration with ML Models

Data exfiltration—Data theft, often referred to as data exportation or data extrusion, is the deliberate, illegal, and secret movement of data from a computer or other device. Malware may be used to automate data exfiltration or it can be done manually.

Data exfiltration attacks are one of the most harmful and disruptive cybersecurity risks, affecting targets that range from regular people to large corporations and governmental organizations. Protecting corporate data and preventing data exfiltration are essential for a number of reasons:

Maintaining business continuity: Data exfiltration can cause financial losses, interfere with operations, and erode consumer confidence.

Complying with regulations: Regulations pertaining to data privacy and protection are particular to several businesses. Data exfiltration frequently arises from or reveals a violation of these rules, and it can result in harsh sanctions and long-term harm to one's reputation.

Safeguarding intellectual property: Research and development, trade secrets, and other sensitive information vital to a company's profitability and competitive edge might be jeopardized via data exfiltration.

Sensitive data is a very desirable target for hackers. Social security numbers, personally identifiable information (PII), stolen customer data, and other private information may be traded on the black market. Additionally, the stolen data may be kept prisoner in a ransomware attack or used to carry out other hacks in return for astronomical payments. (IBM, 2024)

Data exfiltration versus data leakage versus data breach

Data leakage, data breach, and data exfiltration are distinct, albeit related, concepts that are frequently used interchangeably.

The unintentional disclosure of private information is known as data leakage. A technological security flaw or a procedural security issue may cause data to leak.

Any security event that allows unauthorized access to private or sensitive data is referred to as a data breach. Sensitive information is obtained by someone who shouldn't have it.

The discrete act of data theft is known as data exfiltration. While not all data breaches or leaks result in data exfiltration, all data exfiltration necessitates a data leak or breach. For instance, a threat actor may decide to use the data to take over an executive's email account or encrypt it as part of a ransomware operation. Until the data is duplicated or transferred to another storage device that the attacker controls, it is not considered data exfiltration.

The difference matters. Although there isn't much information regarding the price of data exfiltration, a Google search for "data exfiltration costs" usually yields broad information about the expenses of data breaches. These frequently include large ransom payments to stop the sale or disclosure of stolen data as well as further ransoms to stop any future assaults.

How does data exfiltration happen?

- **Usually, data exfiltration is caused by**

    - **An outside attacker—** a foreign opponent, hacker, cybercriminal, or another malevolent actor

    - **A careless insider threat**—an authorized user, such as an employee or business partner, who unintentionally exposes data due to human error, bad judgment (such as falling for a phishing scam), or a lack of knowledge about security measures, rules, and best practices. For instance, there is a risk when someone transfers private information to an insecure device, such as a USB flash drive or portable hard drive.

Rarely, an insider threat—a malevolent person with authorized access to the network, such a dissatisfied employee—is the reason.

Common data exfiltration techniques and attack vectors

Malicious insiders and outside attackers take use of technological security flaws and negligent or undertrained insiders to gain access to and steal confidential information.

Phishing and other social engineering attacks

Social engineering assaults take use of human psychology to coerce or deceive a person into jeopardizing the security of their organization or themselves.

Phishing is the most prevalent kind of social engineering assault, which involves using phone, text, or email messages that pretend to be from a reliable source in order to persuade recipients to take any of the following activities:

- Download harmful software, such ransomware

- Click on links to dubious websites

- Provide personal data, including login credentials

- Give the adversary the data they wish to steal directly

Phishing assaults include highly personalized spear phishing, whale phishing, and business email compromise (BEC) attacks, as well as generic mass phishing communications that seem to be from reputable companies or organizations. BEC attacks use messages purporting to be from superiors or close coworkers to target certain people.

Social engineering, however, may be far less technological. Baiting is a social engineering approach that involves simply placing a thumb drive infected with malware where a person is likely to pick it up. Another method, known as tailgating, is just following a legitimate user into a room or other physical area where data is kept.

Vulnerability exploits

A vulnerability exploit exploits a security hole or weakness in the firmware, software, or hardware of a system or device. Zero-day exploits attack security vulnerabilities that hackers find before software or device providers are aware of them or have the means to address them. In order to circumvent firewall protections and establish a virtual tunnel for the purpose of exfiltrating confidential data, DNS tunneling leverages domain name service (DNS) queries.

The cost of data exfiltration

Exfiltrated data can have expensive repercussions for individuals, including identity theft, bank or credit card fraud, and extortion or blackmail. The repercussions are orders of magnitude more expensive for businesses, especially those in highly regulated sectors like healthcare and banking. Here are some of examples of potential outcomes:

- Operations were disrupted as a result of losing vital company information.

- loss of business or the trust of customers

- Trade secrets that have been compromised include manufacturing techniques, special application codes, and product innovations.

- Serious fines, levies, and other penalties imposed by the government on businesses that must follow stringent privacy and data security guidelines while handling sensitive client information

- Attacks that follow that are enabled by the stolen information

Although it is hard to locate reports or studies of expenditures directly related to data exfiltration, the number of data exfiltration occurrences is rising quickly. The majority of ransomware assaults nowadays are double-extortion operations, in which the hacker encrypts and then steals the victim's data. The cybercriminal then requests a ransom to unlock the data so the victim may start their company again, and further ransoms to stop the data from being sold or made available to outside parties.

In 2020 alone, hundreds of millions of consumer records were stolen by fraudsters from Facebook and Microsoft. In 2022, the hacker collective Lapsus$ stole one terabyte of private information from Nvidia, a semiconductor manufacturer, and released the source code for its deep learning system. The funds used for data exfiltration must be good and improving if hackers follow the money.

Data exfiltration prevention

To stop data exfiltration, organizations employ a mix of security technologies and best practices.

Security awareness training. The prevalence of phishing as a data exfiltration attack vector means that educating users to spot phishing schemes can assist prevent hackers from attempting data exfiltration. Organizations may lower their risk of data exfiltration by educating people on safe password usage, remote work best practices, work-related personal device use, and how to handle, transport, and store corporate data.

Identity and access management (IAM). IAM solutions enable businesses to provide each user on the network a unique digital identity and set of access rights. These solutions prevent hackers and unauthorized users while streamlining access for authorized users. The following technologies can be combined with IAM:

- In addition to a username and password, multi-factor authentication requires one or more log-on credentials.

- Role-based access control (RBAC)—granting access rights according to a user's position within the company.

- Requiring users to reauthenticate when context changes, such as when they transfer devices or try to access highly sensitive apps or data, is known as adaptive authentication.

- Using a single set of login credentials, single sign-on allows users to access several connected on-premises or Cloud services during a session without having to log in again.

Data loss prevention (DLP). DLP systems look for indications of exfiltration in sensitive data while it is in use (being processed), in motion (moving across the network), or at rest (in storage) and block it appropriately. DLP technology, for instance, can prevent data from being processed by an unauthorized program (such as an app a user downloads from the internet) or transferred to an unauthorized Cloud storage provider.

Threat detection and response technologies. User behaviour and business network traffic are continually monitored and analyzed by an expanding class of cybersecurity technology. With the use of these technologies, overworked security teams may identify cyber threats in real-time or almost real-time and react with little manual involvement. Among these technologies are the following:

1. Intrusion detection systems (IDSs)

2. Intrusion prevention systems (IPSs)

3. Security information and event management (SIEM)

4. Security orchestration, automation, and response (SOAR) software

5. Endpoint detection and response (EDR)

6. Extended detection and response (XDR) solutions

Types of machine learning models

Machine learning is dominated by two problem types: prediction and categorization. Models created from algorithms intended for either regression (a technique used for predictive modeling) or classification can be utilized to tackle these issues. Sometimes, depending on how it is trained, the same method may be used to create either regression or classification models.

Examine the list of well-known methods for building regression and classification models that follows.

Machine learning classification models

- Logistic regression
- Naive Bayes
- Decision trees
- Random forest
- K-nearest neighbour (KNN)
- Support vector machine

Machine learning regression models

- Linear regression
- Ridge regression
- Decision trees
- Random forest
- K-nearest neighbour (KNN)
- Neural network regression

4.7 Deep Learning Approaches for Database Access Control

A kind of machine learning called "deep learning" models intricate patterns in data by using artificial neural networks. Deep learning methods work especially well with unstructured data, including text and pictures. Important deep learning strategies consist of:

- **Convolutional Neural Networks (CNNs):** Primarily used for image recognition, CNNs can also analyze visual data related to cyber security, such as graphical representations of network traffic.

- **Recurrent Neural Networks (RNNs):** RNNs are appropriate for jobs like forecasting future occurrences based on time-series data, such as seeing patterns in network assaults over time, because they are made for sequential data processing.

- **Generative Adversarial Networks (GANs):** GANs consist of two neural networks that compete against each other, generating new data samples. In cyber security, GANs can be used to simulate potential attack scenarios or create synthetic datasets for model training.

Deep learning approaches offer powerful capabilities for predictive analytics, particularly when dealing with intricate and high-dimensional data.

In order to comprehend predictive analytics, one must be aware of its fundamental ideas—data collection, analysis, and modeling—as well as the range of methodologies used, from sophisticated machine learning and deep learning techniques to more conventional statistical methods. When combined, these approaches give businesses the resources they need to proactively detect and address cyber threats.

4.8 AI for Automated Patch Management

The cybersecurity industry is not an exception to how artificial intelligence (AI) is transforming many industries. AI's quick development has made it a key factor in determining how cybersecurity will develop in the future. The demand for AI-driven patch management has grown as businesses work to secure their systems and sensitive data from the constantly shifting threat landscape.

Traditional cybersecurity methods previously depended on detection technologies based on signatures and manual labour. It is crucial to recognize, nevertheless, that the reactive strategy was failing to keep up with the growing complexity. New and unidentified dangers were slipping through the holes, and cybercriminals were becoming more cunning. The cybersecurity community, desiring a proactive and dynamic defence approach, then resorted to AI-driven solutions.

The topic of AI-driven patch management will be covered in further detail in this blog. It will be discussed how important it is to keeping a safe and effective computer environment.

What is Patch Management?

An essential procedure for guaranteeing computer systems' security, dependability, and peak performance is patch management. To put it briefly, it is finding, testing, releasing, and installing software patches or updates to fix flaws or vulnerabilities that already exist or to add new features and security improvements.

The Patch Management Process

Patch management is made up of a number of crucial procedures that work together to handle software patches efficiently. These actions consist of:

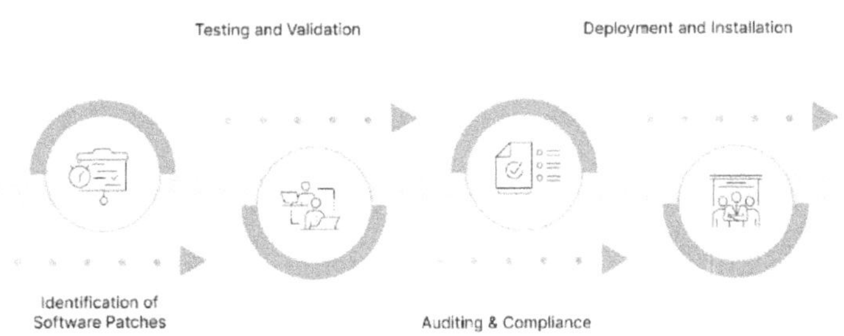

Source: - *(Trackier, 2024)*

1. **Identification of Software Patches:**

   Identifying available software patches tailored to the operating systems, applications, and software components in use is the initial stage in patch management. To fix known problems, increase functionality, and strengthen security, software makers frequently release patches. Usually, reliable sources are used in the identification process, including automatic patch management systems, vendor alerts, and security warnings.

2. **Testing and Validation:**

   Software patches go through a critical testing and validation step when they are detected. Patches are tested in a controlled setting, frequently on a test set of computers, to make sure they don't cause any new problems or conflicts with already-installed software. This testing stage reduces the possibility of applying fixes that can interfere with system functionality or jeopardize security.

3. **Deployment and Installation:**

   Once testing is completed successfully, fixes are prepared for release. To distribute the fixes throughout the network or individual systems, patch management software or manual procedures are employed. By enabling uniform and effective patch delivery, automated deployment technologies cut down on the time and effort needed for human installs. Managing system restarts, planning downtime, and making sure fixes are installed on all pertinent computers are some possible steps in the deployment process.

4. **Auditing and Compliance:**

   Maintaining network visibility and compliance after fixes have been released and implemented is crucial. To make sure that all systems have gotten the required updates, auditing and reporting tools are essential for evaluating patch compliance. Organisations can quickly implement remedial actions by identifying any gaps or irregularities in the patching process through routine audits.

Major Benefits of AI-Driven Patch Management in Cybersecurity

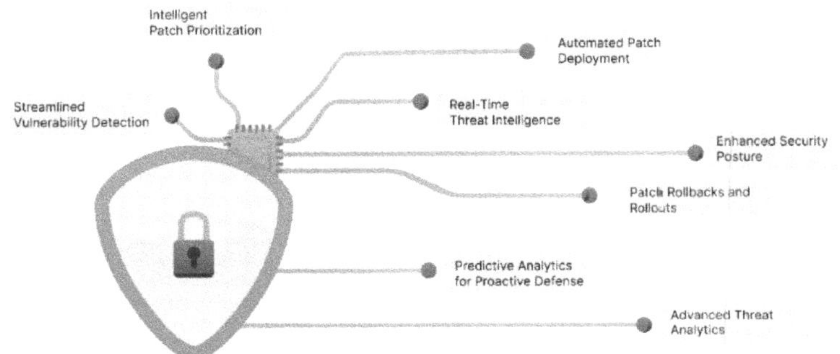

Source: - *(Daffodil, 2023)*

1. **Streamlined Vulnerability Detection:** Through process simplification, AI-driven patch management significantly improves vulnerability detection. AI-powered systems analyze enormous volumes of data using sophisticated machine learning algorithms rather than depending on human labour to find vulnerabilities. This makes it possible to quickly and precisely identify possible weaknesses that hackers may take advantage of. The danger of data breaches and other cyberattacks can be decreased by organisations taking prompt action to remediate vulnerabilities that are proactively identified. You get an automatic and watchful helper that continuously checks your systems with AI-driven patch management, providing you piece of mind and guaranteeing the security of your digital assets.

2. **Intelligent Patch Prioritization:** The capacity of AI-driven patch management to strategically prioritize fixes is one of its main advantages. Critical vulnerabilities go untreated because traditional patch management techniques frequently have trouble deciding which fixes should be applied first. AI-driven systems, on the other hand, rank patches according to their importance by analyzing a

number of variables, such as exploitability, possible effect, and severity. By ensuring that resources are directed where they are most needed, this clever prioritization lowers the attack surface of the company and successfully mitigates possible risks. Consider it as having an experienced counsel who assists you in determining key priorities so that you can concentrate your efforts where they will have the greatest influence.

3. **Real-Time Threat Intelligence:** AI-powered patch management solutions provide real-time threat intelligence by continually collecting and analyzing data from several sources. This implies that you get the most recent knowledge about the newest dangers and methods of assault. Organisations may strengthen their defences, quickly install pertinent fixes, and proactively respond to new threats by utilising this dynamic knowledge. It's similar to having a specialised cybersecurity analyst who keeps an eye on the online environment and updates you on the continuously shifting danger scenario. You remain ahead of the game with AI-driven patch management, which makes sure that your security protocols are constantly in line with the state of threats.

4. **Predictive Analytics for Proactive Defense:** Patch management powered by AI does more than merely fix existing problems. Predictive analytics is used to foresee and stop potential problems. Artificial intelligence (AI) systems may spot any flaws in your systems before they can be used against you by examining past data, trends, and behaviours. Organisations are empowered by this proactive strategy to take preventative actions before cyber risks manifest, such as patching vulnerabilities, putting security measures in place, or altering configurations. It's similar to having a crystal ball that can identify any weaknesses in your systems so you can take preventative measures and avoid danger.

5. **Automated Patch Deployment:** Manual patch deployment procedures can be resource-intensive, time-consuming, and prone

to errors. On the other hand, patch distribution is automated via AI-driven patch management, which makes it dependable and effective. The solution reduces the possibility of human mistake and saves significant time and money by identifying vulnerabilities, prioritizing updates, and smoothly deploying them across your systems. Your cybersecurity team may concentrate on high-level security activities and strategic goals by automating the technical parts of patch administration. It's similar to having a reliable helper do the tiresome and repetitive parts of patch deployment, freeing up your team to work more strategically and efficiently.

6. **Enhanced Security Posture:** Improving an organization's overall security posture is mostly dependent on AI-driven patch management. Through the use of intelligent patch prioritization, automated patch distribution, and simplified vulnerability identification, organisations may drastically minimize their attack surface. By strengthening defences and minimizing vulnerabilities, this all-encompassing strategy lowers the likelihood of data breaches and cyberattacks. A strong security posture gives your stakeholders, partners, and consumers' confidence in addition to safeguarding your digital assets. AI-driven patch management lays a solid basis for a cybersecurity infrastructure that is durable and powerful.

7. **Patch Rollbacks and Rollouts:** AI-driven patch management offers intelligent capabilities for patch rollbacks and rollouts in addition to patch deployment. AI systems can automatically start patch rollbacks to restore system stability if a patch results in unforeseen problems or disputes. By doing this, companies may minimize interruptions and preserve operational continuity by promptly addressing any unforeseen repercussions of patch release. AI-driven solutions, on the other hand, may intelligently roll out patches throughout the organization's infrastructure when new fixes are judged safe and prepared for deployment, guaranteeing reliable and effective patch implementation. AI-driven patch management provides improved control and flexibility with these intelligent rollback and rollout

tools, enabling businesses to successfully handle unanticipated situations while preserving a safe environment.

8. **Advanced Threat Analytics and Forensics:** AI-driven patch management incorporates advanced threat analytics and forensics capabilities to go beyond patch deployment and vulnerability identification. Through constant examination of user activity, network traffic, and system behaviour, artificial intelligence (AI) systems are able to spot and identify possible indications of security breaches or malicious activity. By enabling proactive detection and response, this sophisticated threat analytics gives organisations real-time information into possible attacks.

AI-driven patch management systems may also do forensic analysis in the case of a security incident to determine the scope of the breach, look into the underlying cause, and assist with incident response activities. By strengthening an organization's capacity to identify, reduce, and recover from security events, these sophisticated analytics and forensics capabilities guarantee thorough protection of vital assets and infrastructure.

Safeguard Your Digital Assets

The potential effects of AI-driven patch management are endless as we move forward. The window of opportunity for cyberattacks will be much reduced as a result of developments in machine learning algorithms, which will allow systems to automatically detect and fix flaws in real time. Organizations are able to remain ahead of the constantly shifting threat landscape thanks to this proactive strategy.

All set to improve your defence tactics? Learn more about our cutting-edge AI development services. Take use of artificial intelligence's proactive protection capabilities and make sure your digital infrastructure is resilient. Rely on our experience to handle the intricacies of the changing threat scenario.

4.9 Chapter Summary

This chapter discusses several other advanced techniques regarding cybersecurity and focuses on the role of AI as well as deep learning. Today threat prevention has transited from simple perimeter protection techniques to a more complex approach with layers of protection. Application such as Next Generation Firewalls (NGFWs), and Mobile device security validates the coverage in question. Escalating threats for cyber security is solved by machine learning (ML) and AI as they participate in automation of tasks, increase scalability, and reach new types of threats. With such challenges as data quality and adversarial attacks, ML creates predictions and dynamic threat counteraction. Such deep learning methods as CNNs, RNNs, and GANs are of great importance in cyber security along with other involved large-scale data analysis.

The chapter also raises awareness of data exfiltration as among the biggest dangers to an organization, including too sensitive data. The solutions like security awareness training, identity and access management, advanced detection system can protect organizations against data theft. Finally, artificial intelligence-based patch management software updates, incorporating identification of vulnerable areas, testing-containers, deployment, and compliance review. Such undertakings make it possible to automate several processes required in the protection against increasingly sophisticated cyber threats, and steady security and operations. The chapter insist on the harmonious cooperation of humans and AI because the knowledge derived from experience is still pertinent in providing context and maintaining appropriate ethical standard in generating threat intelligence with AI. Combined, they are a preventive, active type of protection for digital environments and platforms.

Multiple-choice questions (MCQs)

1. **Why is threat prevention crucial in cybersecurity?**

    a. It ensures faster data transfers

    b. It minimizes the risk of damage by addressing potential threats before they cause harm

    c. It focuses only on detecting attacks after they occur

    d. It reduces the cost of hardware maintenance

2. **How does machine learning contribute to preventing database attacks?**

    a. By identifying and blocking harmful traffic based on patterns and anomalies in real-time

    b. By encrypting database records

    c. By storing data in multiple databases

    d. By increasing system hardware capacity

3. **What is the main advantage of predictive analytics in threat mitigation?**

    a. It improves the speed of network connections

    b. It forecasts potential security threats based on historical data and trends, allowing for proactive defense

    c. It stores historical data for later use

    d. It generates real-time network traffic reports

4. **What does threat intelligence sharing powered by AI enable?**

    a. The exchange of data on known threats and vulnerabilities to improve collective security

    b. The sharing of financial information between organizations

    c. The secure storage of private data

    d. The automatic patching of vulnerabilities in systems

5. **How can machine learning models help prevent data exfiltration?**

   a. By detecting unusual patterns in data transfer and blocking unauthorized data access or leakage

   b. By encrypting data during transfer

   c. By slowing down data transfer to prevent loss

   d. By storing data in secure physical locations

6. **What is the purpose of using deep learning approaches for database access control?**

   a. To manually verify every user request for database access

   b. To automatically adapt and learn to distinguish between legitimate and suspicious access attempts based on user behavior

   c. To store passwords securely in the database

   d. To optimize database performance

7. **How does AI improve the process of automated patch management?**

   a. By identifying vulnerabilities and automatically applying patches or updates to prevent exploitation

   b. By increasing the speed of patch downloads

   c. By reducing the need for system backups

   d. By creating new versions of software to replace outdated ones

8. **In what way does machine learning contribute to mitigating database attacks?**

   a. By generating random passwords for users

   b. By analyzing past attack patterns and predicting potential future threats, enabling early intervention

   c. By providing users with personalized security alerts

   d. By encrypting database queries in real-time

9. **What does AI-powered predictive analytics do in threat prevention?**

    a. It analyzes network traffic to identify patterns of potential attacks

    b. It monitors database performance to ensure efficient operations

    c. It automatically backs up sensitive data

    d. It focuses only on protecting hardware resources

10. **Why is AI crucial for preventing data exfiltration in modern databases?**

    a. It improves the physical security of data storage devices

    b. It learns from data access patterns to detect and block unauthorized data transfers in real-time

    c. It reduces the size of data backups

    d. It secures the physical access to the database servers

Answers

1	2	3	4	5	6	7	8	9	10
B	A	B	A	A	B	A	B	A	B

RECENT DEVELOPMENTS IN CLOUD DATABASE SECURITY

5.1 Chapter Overview

The modern development of Cloud database security responds to the modern threats posed by Various strategies for privacy and data security in sophisticated and distributed computing. Federated learning has been recognized as a secure method of data processing, on the one hand. together without revealing the information to third parties, while, on the other hand, AI-assisted multi-Cloud security solutions improve overall threat identification and compliance with the rules in different Clouds. Through records space and innovative smart contracts, blockchain technology is revolutionizing the ways of ensuring secure Cloud computing. By far the most significant development in secure data sharing over the last decade has been homomorphic encryption that enables the processing of encrypted data without decryption, thereby maintaining confidentiality right from the data generation stage and throughout their usage lifecycle. Insider threat detection is implemented through artificial intelligence, which uses machine learning algorithms to analyze user activity and identify dangers within organizations. Innovations in edge computing security enhance Cloud databases since it shields data synchronization, processes lightweight encryption, and adapts zero-trust principles that mitigate risks in the distributed structure. Altogether, these innovations are shifting the Cloud database security that has been becoming smarter, more refined and more elaborate to meet modern challenges.

5.2 Advances in Federated Learning for Secure Data Processing

A central server and a collection of clients are involved in the distributed machine-learning method known as federated learning (FL). Computing nodes known as clients use their local data to conduct local training. Initially, a collection of clients receives a standard global model from the central server. After that, clients use local data to train the global model and return local models to the server. After combining the local models into a new global model, the server initiates a fresh training cycle. Until the global model converges or a certain threshold is met, this procedure may be carried out several times.

The two main FL categories—cross-device and cross-silo—depend on the kind of clients being utilized. In cross-device FL, a standard global model is trained by storing all training data locally on several devices with erratic and restricted network connections, such smartphones or Internet of Things devices. The architecture of cross-device FL must therefore take into account the frequent joining and dropping out of FL clients.

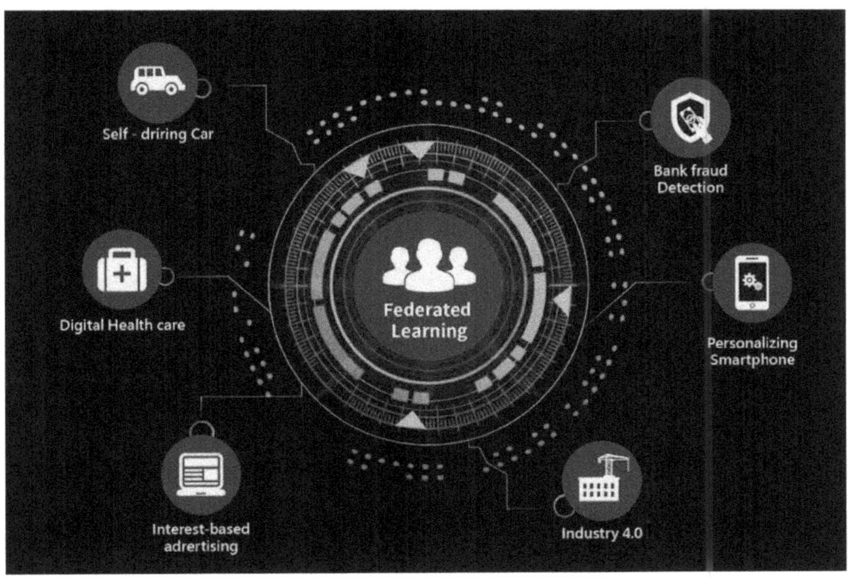

Source: - *(Hacks, 2024)*

Conversely, cross-silo FL uses datasets spread across many organizations and geo-distributed data centers to train a global model. Because of data protection laws, operational difficulties (such data duplication and synchronization), or expensive expenses, certain datasets are not allowed to leave organizations or data centre areas. Cross-silo FL, as opposed to cross-device FL, makes the assumption that businesses or data centers have dependable network connections, strong computer capabilities, and accessible datasets.

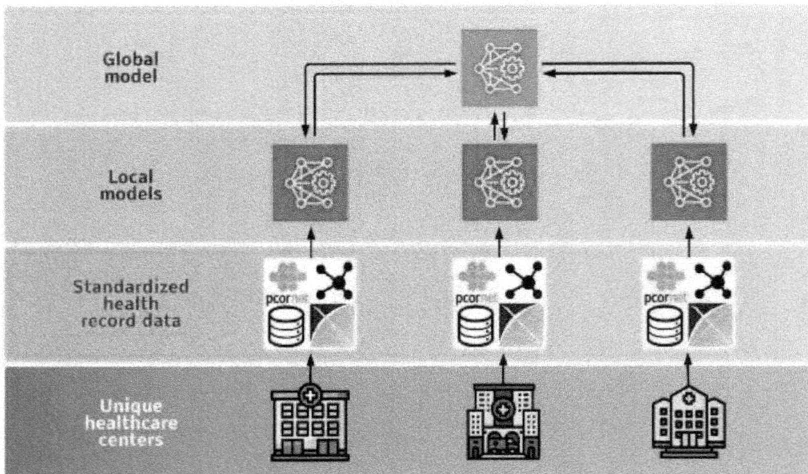

Source: - *(Hacks, 2024)*

Federated learning is essentially a collaborative machine learning method that uses local data samples to train an algorithm across several servers or devices without ever sharing the actual data. In situations where access rights, security, and data privacy present serious obstacles, this idea is revolutionary. Imagine a world in which devices learn from user behaviour to improve features without sacrificing privacy, or where hospitals can work together to improve patient outcomes using sophisticated AI models without disclosing sensitive patient data. These situations are becoming a reality thanks to federated learning.

The most important benefit of federated learning is its capacity to safeguard data and user privacy. Sensitive information is less likely to be exposed during transmission or storage since the raw data never leaves its originating device. This component is especially important for adhering to strict data protection laws like the GDPR in Europe ('Hacks, 2024).

Fundamentals of Federated Learning

- **Decentralized Model Training:** In federated learning, only model updates (gradients) are sent to a central server or aggregator; model training is done locally on each device using its own data. This decentralized method protects data privacy and reduces the need for data transit.

- **Secure Aggregation:** Federated learning uses safe aggregation techniques, such homomorphic encryption and differential privacy, to aggregate model updates from many devices while maintaining privacy. These methods guarantee that private data is safeguarded during the model aggregation procedure.

- **Asynchronous Communication:** Federated learning supports asynchronous communication between devices and the central server, allowing devices to participate in model training at their own pace. This flexibility enables federated learning to accommodate devices with varying computational capabilities and network conditions.

Advanced Techniques in Federated Learning

- **Federated Averaging:** To update the global model, federated averaging, a fundamental method in federated learning, collects model updates from several devices. Federated averaging produces a globally optimized model by averaging the updates while accounting for variations in data distribution and device participation. Example Implementation: Federated Averaging in TensorFlow.

- **Adaptive Client Selection:** To improve the efficiency and convergence speed of federated learning, adaptive client selection techniques dynamically select a subset of devices for model training based on their data characteristics and model performance. This ensures that devices with informative data contribute more to the training process.

- **Personalized Federated Learning:** Personalized federated learning tailors the global model to individual devices or user preferences by incorporating device-specific updates during model aggregation. This enables personalized recommendations, predictive maintenance, and other customized services while preserving privacy.

Applications of Federated Learning

- **Mobile Health Monitoring:**

  In order to create individualized health monitoring and diagnostic models while safeguarding sensitive health data, federated learning allows cooperative model training on smartphone devices. By leveraging data from diverse sources, federated learning improves model generalization and accuracy.

- **Edge AI and IoT:**

  Federated learning enables on-device model training and inference in edge computing and IoT contexts. This enables intelligent edge applications like anomaly detection and predictive maintenance by enabling edge devices to learn from local sensor data and adjust to changing surroundings in real-time.

- **Privacy-Preserving Analytics:**

  Through the localization of sensitive data on user devices and the privacy-preserving aggregation of model updates, federated learning guarantees data confidentiality and privacy. For privacy-sensitive applications like financial analytics and behavioral analysis, this makes federated learning appropriate (Malaviarachchi, 2024).

  To apply federated learning for edge computing that protects privacy, do these crucial actions:

1. **Set Up the Environment**: Set up Cloud servers, edge servers, and edge devices to cooperate seamlessly.

2. **Prepare Data**: Distribute information across devices, protect it, and prepare it for training.

3. **Initialize the Model**: Configure the global model, deploy it to edge devices, and select the appropriate architecture and configuration.

4. **Train Local Models**: Enhance local model performance, protect data, and train models on edge devices.

5. **Aggregate Model Updates**: Utilize methods such as Differential Privacy and Secure Multi-Party Computation to safely combine local model changes.

6. **Update the Global Model**: Send the updated model to devices, combine local updates, and maintain the security of the global model.

7. **Evaluate and Monitor**: Evaluate system performance, keep an eye on security and privacy, and troubleshoot and optimize the system.

Federated learning provides an effective and efficient way to train models while protecting privacy as data creation at the edge increases. Future plans call for increasing model accuracy, decreasing communication overhead, scalability, and integrating with other edge technologies.

Privacy in Distributed Computing

Edge computing and other distributed computing systems provide privacy concerns. There is a chance of data breaches or abuse when information is exchanged between devices or forwarded to central servers.

Federated learning solves these issues by removing the necessity for data sharing and maintaining data localization on devices. According to data protection laws, this decentralized method guarantees that private and sensitive information stays safe.

Preparing Data

Distributing Data Across Devices

In federated learning, the dataset should be divided into smaller portions and sent to other devices for local model training. There are several methods for doing this:

- **Horizontal partitioning**: Divide the dataset according to rows or samples into smaller portions.

- **Vertical partitioning**: Using columns or characteristics, divide the dataset into smaller portions.

- **Hybrid partitioning**: Use both vertical and horizontal splitting to effectively disperse data.

To preserve model correctness, ensure that each device receives a representative sample of the dataset when the data is divided.

Keeping Data Private and Secure

In federated learning, safeguarding data security and privacy is essential. Here are some of tactics:

- **Data encryption**: To avoid unwanted access, encrypt data before transferring it to devices.

- **Access control**: Limit data access to just authorized individuals and devices.

- **Anonymization**: Eliminate user IDs and sensitive information from the data.

Using these techniques guarantees that data is kept confidential and safe during the federated learning process.

Preparing Data for Training

The data must be preprocessed before the model is trained:

- **Data cleaning**: Eliminate noisy data, outliers, and missing values from the dataset.

- **Feature engineering**: To enhance the model's performance, extract pertinent characteristics from the dataset.

- **Data normalization**: Data should be normalized to avoid feature dominance and guarantee consistent scalability.

Effective data preprocessing can lower the chance of data breaches and enhance model performance (Chen & Cui, 2024).

5.3 AI-Powered Multi-Cloud Security Solutions

Multi-Cloud is considered the standard ecosystem for enterprises across the globe today and provides improvements in scalability, flexibility, and overall operation. However, the implementation of multi-cloud environments creates ample security issues, including disparities in security policies and compliance degrees as well as increased threat environments. There are innovative technologies for these challenges that can be offered with the help of AI to guarantee comprehensive security for modern Cloud platforms.

Despite the many advantages of multi-cloud techniques, they also present new difficulties, especially with regard to security. Managing and protecting workloads, data, and apps across several Cloud platforms may be extremely difficult. Asset protection in a multi-cloud ecosystem is a challenge for traditional security solutions, which are frequently created for on-premise systems or single-cloud settings. Artificial Intelligence (AI) is transforming how businesses handle Cloud security in this situation. With AI's capacity to learn, adapt, and handle massive volumes of data in real-time, there are now more chances than ever before to protect multi-cloud settings. This extensive blog will explore how artificial intelligence (AI) may improve multi-cloud security, including important topics like automation, real-time analytics, identity management, enhanced threat detection, and compliance.

The Role of AI in Transforming Multi-Cloud Security

As it comes to protecting multi-cloud settings, artificial intelligence (AI) has changed the game by providing capabilities that go well beyond those of conventional security solutions. Conventional technologies can only identify known risks since they are reactive and rule-based, even if they work well in on-premise and single-cloud settings. But in a dynamic multi-cloud environment where threats are always changing, this reactive strategy is no longer adequate. AI fills this gap by analyzing massive datasets from various Cloud settings in real-time using machine learning algorithms, which enables proactive, predictive threat identification. AI technologies are especially good at identifying trends and actions that point to possible security lapses, enabling businesses to take action before any harm is done. Additionally, companies may have unified insight across all of their Cloud platforms with AI-driven solutions. Because every Cloud service provider has different security procedures, tools, and configurations, managing security in a multi-cloud environment is challenging. Security teams can handle threats from a single dashboard thanks to AI's centralized control and monitoring, which streamlines this complexity. By resolving disparities in security procedures among various Cloud providers, helps to maintain the security of all settings. Regular security duties may also be automated by AI, which lowers human error and frees up IT professionals to work on more important projects. To put it briefly, artificial intelligence (AI) is essential to changing multi-cloud security by making it more clever, responsive, and effective.

The Future of AI in Multi-Cloud Security

The importance of AI in Cloud security will only increase with the growing use of multi-cloud settings. Organizations' capacity to protect their multi-cloud environments will be further improved by developments in AI technology, such as the creation of increasingly complex machine learning algorithms and the combination of AI and quantum computing. AI-powered security systems will grow more independent in the future, able to identify and address threats without the need for human assistance. Additionally, AI will become more predictive, allowing businesses to foresee possible security threats and take action before an attack happens. This will be particularly crucial as fraudsters keep creating increasingly sophisticated methods to take advantage of weaknesses in Cloud settings. In order to assist organizations, keep ahead of new risks, AI-driven solutions will also be crucial in the creation of new security standards and procedures. Businesses will be in a better position to protect their multi-cloud systems from future threats if they invest in AI-driven security solutions now. Businesses may build more robust, secure Cloud infrastructures that can adjust to the constantly shifting cybersecurity landscape by utilizing AI(Kuriakose, 2024).

- **Multi-Cloud:** Core Stack bridges the feature gap between cost, security, operations, and compliance by improving and expanding native Cloud capabilities, regardless of whether you support AWS, Azure, GCP, OCI, or a mix of Clouds.

- **AI-Powered:** AI is used by the Core stack platform to not only manage the Cloud lifecycle but also to offer insightful analysis and forecasts on your Cloud usage.

Key Features of AI-Powered Multi-Cloud Security Solutions

1. Threat Detection and Reaction in Real Time A set of algorithms known as artificial intelligence (AI) can analyze data in real time and identify security threats. For instance, the machine learning language can detect abnormal traffic patterns that characterize DDoS attacks or data leakage. They reduce threats before severe losses are done through fast identification by AI and the trending of automatic responses. As stated by J et al., 2023 AI-based anomaly detection decreases the time to detect threats by up to 85 percent from conventional approaches.

2. Management of Unified Security AI makes it possible to apply a single security policy across several Clouds and to completely synchronize the rules applied across all Cloud platforms. This minimizes the challenge of dealing with several vendors because there will be conformity on the aspect of security. Referring to the study, it was found that companies that use AI-based multi-cloud management solutions gain a 30% increase in regulations' effectiveness.

3. A Predictive Analytics AI uses the concept of predictive analysis to foresee some possible security threats within the firm by examining previous data and new threats. This capability enables organizations

to take pre-emptive measures on security and control the gaps that hackers might explore. In a survey conducted by (Rakibul Hasan Chowdhury et al., 2024), deployment of predictive analytics employing Artificial Intelligence decreased cyberattack success rates by 40%.

4. Automated Monitoring of Compliance with regulations like the CCPA, GDPR, and HIPAA is essential for businesses operating in multi-cloud settings. These solutions put into practice the principles of artificial intelligence to continuously check and enforce compliance with regulatory standards. According to (Akitra, 2024), the use of AI-based automation allows companies to reduce compliance check costs by 40 percent per year in auditing.

Challenges in Implementing AI-Powered Multi-Cloud Security

1. Data Privacy Issues Due to the power and operation of other artificial intelligence models that require massive dataset, data privacy becomes an issue. Preserving user data and yet utilizing strong artificial intelligence is still an issue of concern.

2. Integration Complexity Generally, incorporation of AI solutions into current complex multi-cloud structures is not easy and easily could take a lot of resources and time.

3. Security Benefits That said, there are several costs inherent with implementing AI that must be considered, especially by organizations that are small to mid-sized.

The Benefits of AI-Powered Multi-Cloud Security

1. Better incident prioritization Incident response teams receive numerous alerts, and most of them are noisy or potentially not real threats. The AI system helps to categorize risks to prioritize the threats according to the extent of their danger. From here it allows security teams to prioritise addressing the most critical vulnerabilities.

Example: Newer AI solutions rely on NLP to navigate through logs and reports, and offer key findings to the user.

2. Dynamic Security Adaptation AI refines the effectual and efficient security paradigms by learning from topographical chaos. Whereas the rule-based approach can be rigid and become ineffective thinking of new attack approaches AI is dynamic in responding to new cases.

3. Granular Data Protection AI allows organizations to leverage even the most complex data protection tools that have dynamic data masking and encryption to meet the unique needs of the Cloud environment. Many firms that operate in the ability of AI to dynamically safeguard customer data would be beneficial to highly regulated areas like banking and healthcare.

4. Cross Cloud Orchestration AI enforces strong security policies across different Clouds in a single environment and avails information on policy alignment to different Clouds without incurring the risk of losing compatibility with the selected Cloud sold by different companies. The reason for this unification is to eliminate configuration errors – a common factor leading to data breaches.

5. Lower Mean Time to Respond (MTTR) In contrast, applying traditional structures of security may take a long time to counter an incident due to its complex processes. AI optimizes time taken in the incident response lifecycle by performing simple tasks such as identification of threats and controlling or fixing the affected systems.

Use Cases in Multi-Cloud Security

1. Security software in the form of Network Traffic Analysis AI algorithms works in real-time to track traffic across multiple Cloud platforms and identify signs of malicious activity and intrusion. AI can discern normal and suspicious activity and minimize insider threats as well as Advanced Persistent Threats (APT).

2. Security Data First Look Data Loss Prevention (DLP) Data in multi-cloud becomes transportable across Clouds and endpoints. The use of AI uplifts DLP because data becomes protected by detecting and tracking the flow of sensitive data to prevent it from being transferred.

3. AI-based SIEM (Security Information and Event Management) systems gather information from several Clouds, analyze logs, and search for trends that might indicate an intrusion.

4. Workload Protection AI protects workloads in the different Cloud platforms using Behaviour Analysis and Anomaly detection to ensure the protection of applications.

5. Anti-Fraud In areas such as electronic business and finance, artificial intelligence comprehends the abnormal transactions and other similar activities, in applications existing in the Cloud (Nedunoori, 2024).

Top 2 Multi-Cloud Security Solutions in 2025

Security solutions for many Clouds help safeguard your users, rights, and assets. They will make sure that you are not caught off guard by hidden dangers and assist you in meeting compliance criteria. The top ten multi-cloud security solutions for 2025 will be examined based on evaluations and rankings from several reliable sources.

1. Google Cloud Platform

Google Cloud Platform is preferred by a wide range of sectors and multinational corporations because of its flexibility, scalability, and simplicity of use. It supports contemporary corporate undertakings and is among the top award-winning multi-cloud security solutions. It also deploys data efficiently. By utilizing serverless computing settings, it enables companies to develop and migrate applications across various Cloud environments, with an emphasis on providing its tools and services on intelligent infrastructure.

Features:

- Security and compliance measures for delicate tasks

- Cloud Key Management, Cloud IDS, and Cloud Asset Inventory Management

- Encrypts data being used by confidential VMs and delivers hardware key security with HSM

- Firewall insights, audit logging, Cloud-native threat detection, and centralized multi-tenant service access at scale

2. Fugue

Fugue handles Cloud security and compliance for both public and private Clouds using a single policy engine. It provides a centralized view of all Cloud resources and relationships and satisfies compliance both before and after deployment.

Features:

- PCI reporting, monitoring, and self-sufficient Cloud compliance

- Creates security guidelines as code and architecture.

- Complex vulnerability detection, automated misconfiguration cleanup, and tracking of Cloud indicators of compromise (IoCs)

- SIEM tools, log management, and CI/CD pipelines

The best multi-cloud security solution is determined by five parameters:

- **General requirements** – This is determined by the size, market share, number of clients, and partner ecosystems of the business.

- **Functional requirements**– comprises requirements for multi-cloud administration, security, governance, and API capabilities.

- **Customer service and support** – Non-negotiable and requiring round-the-clock customer service for committed help and instruction in utilizing these solutions.

- **Security requirements**– include third-party compliance, disaster recovery, encryption, and business continuity planning.

- **Pricing** – Every company has a budget that it cannot go over when purchasing multi-cloud security solutions (SentinelOne, 2024b).

5.4 The Role of Blockchain in Enhancing Cloud Security

The distributed ledger technology known as blockchain was developed to fortify cryptocurrencies such as Bitcoin. But these days, its uses are far more widespread than simply cryptocurrency. Fundamentally, blockchain is an immutable, decentralized ledger that keeps track of transactions across several computers or nodes. A chain of blocks is created when each transaction, or "block," is linked to the one before it(Paseband & Verisk, 2021).

Since blockchain technology is becoming popular across a wide range of industries, it is typically seen as an incorruptible technology. According to some, blockchain technology can alleviate security issues in Cloud environments. The blockchain's consensus process makes it difficult to erase any transaction data that has been saved. In addition, the hacker finds it more difficult to alter the transaction data. It implies that data modification becomes more challenging as the number of blockchain nodes increases. There is a cost associated with this blockchain solution to the security and legal issues in the Cloud forensic dilemma. Performance expenses increase when blockchain ledgers are widely dispersed. Although these technologies bring benefits to organizations, they also present significant obstacles.

The main advantage of Cloud computing is that it makes company operations more efficient. The advantages of blockchain prioritize security. Blockchain can result in higher performance costs in the Cloud computing environment, despite ensuring data privacy and transaction traceability(Aliyev, 2017).

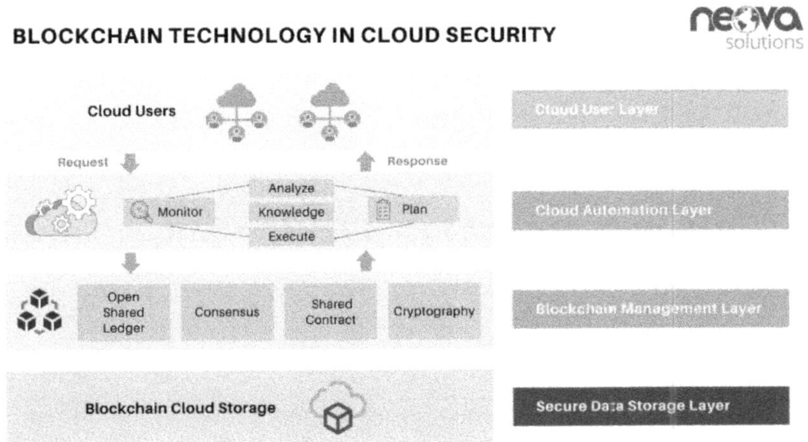

Source: - *(Nagmetulla, 2020)*

Key security benefits of blockchain:

- **Encryption**: Unauthorized users can seldom access or change anything recorded on the blockchain since it is encrypted.

- **Decentralization**: Because blockchain technology is decentralized, it removes single points of failure, which lowers the possibility of data breaches.

- **Consensus Mechanisms**: Blockchain verifies transactions using consensus techniques like Proof of Work (PoW) and Proof of Stake (PoS), guaranteeing that only authorized modifications are made to the ledger.

Key security benefits of blockchain:

- **Encryption**: Unauthorized users can seldom access or change anything recorded on the blockchain since it is encrypted.

- **Decentralization**: Because blockchain technology is decentralized, it removes single points of failure, which lowers the possibility of data breaches.

- **Consensus Mechanisms**: Blockchain verifies transactions using consensus techniques like Proof of Work (PoW) and Proof of Stake (PoS), guaranteeing that only authorized modifications are made to the ledger.

How Blockchain can enhance Cloud Security?

- **Immutable Audit Trails**: Immutability is one of the core characteristics of blockchain technology. Data cannot be changed or removed from the blockchain after it has been recorded there without the consent of all network users. Using this Blockchain feature, an unchangeable audit trail of every action taken in a Cloud environment may be produced. Transparency and accountability are provided by the blockchain's secure access to every modification, access request, and data transfer.

- **Data Integrity Assurance**: Data that is kept in the Cloud may be susceptible to manipulation or illegal access. Organizations may guarantee data integrity by generating cryptographic hashes of their data and depositing them on the blockchain. The stored hash and the recalculated hash will not match if any unauthorized modifications are made to the data, which will cause an alert.

- **Decentralized Identity and Access Management**: Identity management systems built on the blockchain present a strong argument for improving authorization and authentication in Cloud settings. The blockchain allows users to store their self-sovereign identities, which lowers the possibility of identity theft. Additionally, decentralized identification systems provide individuals more control over their personal data and permission to use it.

- **Smart Contracts for Security Policies**: Smart contracts are self-executing agreements that have their terms encoded directly into the code. In Cloud environments, they may be used to automate and enforce security regulations. For example, smart contracts can include access control restrictions to guarantee that only authorized users can access particular Cloud services.

- **Supply Chain Security**: In order to stop harmful code from invading Cloud settings, software supply chains must be secured. By using blockchain technology, software, and upgrades may be transparently and impenetrably recorded, confirming their provenance and validity.

- **Zero Trust Security:** Blockchain technology is compatible with Zero Trust security concepts. Only verified and authorized entities may access Cloud resources thanks to blockchain-based identity and access management, which never assumes trust and maintains constant verification (Paseband & Verisk, 2021).

The Need for Enhanced Cloud Security Measures

Today's Cloud infrastructures are more vulnerable to cyberattacks. Cloud security has become a significant topic due to the increasing frequency and sophistication of assaults. Hackers frequently take advantage of weaknesses, leading to disastrous data breaches.

Current Challenges in Cloud Security

1. **Increased Attack Surface**: As more data and applications move to the Cloud, the potential targets for cybercriminals expand.

2. **Sophisticated Cyber Threats**: Modern attacks employ techniques like Advanced Persistent Threats (APTs) and multi-vector attacks that can bypass traditional security measures.

3. **Insider Threats**: Contractors or employees who have access to private information may unintentionally or purposely provide serious hazards.

4. **Third-party Risks**: Dependence on outside providers for Cloud services may result in more risks if such providers don't have strong security protocols.

Urgency for Stronger Protective Measures

Statistics highlight the urgent need for better security protocols:

- According to an IBM analysis, a data breach in 2021 typically cost $4.24 million.

- According to Gartner, customers will be responsible for 99 percent of Cloud security incidents by 2025, highlighting the need for more user awareness and controls.

Strong security measures must be put in place by organizations to secure their Cloud infrastructures. Blockchain technology offers innovative solutions to many of these challenges, providing a path toward more resilient and trustworthy Cloud security frameworks.

How Blockchain Technology Strengthens Cloud Security

1. **Decentralization for Resilience Against Attacks**: Decentralization is a core principle of blockchain technology that enhances Cloud security. Traditional Cloud architectures often rely on centralized servers, creating a single point of failure. The system as a whole is at danger if this core node is hacked. Blockchain, on the other hand, functions as a decentralized network of nodes, each of which keeps a copy of the ledger. By doing this, the risks connected to central sites of failure are decreased.

2. **Immutability for Trustworthy Audit Trail**: Because of blockchain's immutability, data cannot be changed or removed once it has been recorded. This creates tamper-proof records,

enhancing accountability and providing reliable audit trails essential for regulatory compliance.

3. **Cryptography to Ensure Data Integrity**: Blockchain protects data via cryptographic hashes. By acting as distinct digital fingerprints, these hashes make sure that any unauthorized data alteration is immediately identifiable.

4. **Decentralized Identity Management**: The decentralized identity management made possible by blockchain removes the need for centralized authority when it comes to user authentication. This improves security by dividing control across several nodes and lowers the dangers related to single points of failure.

5. **Smart Contracts as Automated Enforcers**: Self-executing codes with terms built right into software are known as smart contracts. By automating procedures and enforcing security regulations in Cloud settings, they can lessen the need for manual operations and the possibility of mistakes.

6. **Transparency for Compliance**: Blockchain's transparency provides clear advantages for visibility and compliance. Transparent transaction histories enhance data flow visibility, aiding in regulatory compliance by simplifying audit processes (Chain, 2024).

5.5 Secure Data Sharing Through Homomorphic Encryption

A revolutionary cryptographic method called homomorphic encryption enables computation on encrypted material without requiring its decryption. This feature is groundbreaking because it fixes a serious flaw in conventional encryption techniques, which need sensitive data to be decoded before processing can begin, leaving it vulnerable to security breaches.

under an environment where data security and privacy are always under danger, HE provides a means of harnessing the power of data without sacrificing its integrity. Since data is frequently stored and processed remotely in Cloud services, homomorphic encryption is essential for enabling safe calculations (Bhuyan, 2017).

Why is Homomorphic Encryption Important?

As Cloud computing and data-driven decision-making gain popularity, more and more businesses are keeping private data on Cloud servers. Cloud services provide scalability and ease, but there are serious security threats as well. Data breaches can have disastrous effects, including monetary losses and reputational harm.

Because homomorphic encryption keeps sensitive data encrypted across the whole processing cycle, it reduces these dangers. This makes it impossible for a malevolent actor to access the underlying data, even if they manage to get access to the Cloud infrastructure. In the pursuit of compliance with strict data protection laws, HE becomes a crucial facilitator of safe data processing and privacy protection.

The Mechanism of Homomorphic Encryption

The capacity of homomorphic encryption to directly enable mathematical operations on ciphertexts is its fundamental concept. This is a detailed explanation of how homomorphic encryption operates:

Types of Homomorphic Encryption

Three primary categories may be used to classify homomorphic encryption according to the kinds of operations they support:

1. **Partially Homomorphic Encryption (PHE)**

    Only one kind of operation—either addition or multiplication—can be performed on ciphertexts using partially homomorphic encryption. Among the examples are:

    -   **RSA Encryption**: supports multiplicative homomorphism mostly.

- **ElGamal Encryption**: supports multiplicative operations as well.

These methods work well in certain situations but are ineffective in others when more intricate calculations incorporating both kinds of operations are needed.

2. **Fully Homomorphic Encryption (FHE)**

The most flexible kind of homomorphic encryption is fully homomorphic encryption, which permits addition and multiplication operations on ciphertexts.

- **Example**: The first completely homomorphic encryption method was the Gentry method, which Craig Gentry suggested in 2009. Despite its theoretical strength, its computational complexity prevents it from being widely adopted just yet.

FHE is appropriate for applications such as sophisticated data analytics and secure machine learning as it permits arbitrary calculations.

3. **Somewhat Homomorphic Encryption (SHE)**

A certain number of addition and multiplication operations are supported by somewhat homomorphic encryption before the ciphertext's noise renders decryption impossible.

- **Example**: One well-known SHE system is BGV (Brake ski-Gentry-Vaikuntanathan).

She strikes a compromise between functionality and performance in some situations where a small number of actions are sufficient.

Applications of Homomorphic Encryption

There are many opportunities in a variety of industries when encrypted data may be used for calculations. These are some of noteworthy uses for homomorphic encryption:

- **Cloud Computing**

  Cloud computing is one of the most important areas where homomorphic encryption is used. Without disclosing their private information, businesses may contract with Cloud services to handle and store their data. For instance, a healthcare institution can use a Cloud server to store patient records and do analytics without disclosing any private health information.

- **Healthcare**

  Patient confidentiality is of utmost importance in the healthcare industry. Medical personnel may safely share and handle patient data while maintaining the security of sensitive information by using homomorphic encryption. For instance, researchers can work together on patient data to create novel therapies without having access to personally identifiable patient data.

- **Financial Services**

  The banking industry is very regulated and vulnerable to security breaches. Banks and other financial organizations may handle consumer data, evaluate risks, and identify fraud while protecting consumer privacy thanks to homomorphic encryption. Example: Without decrypting the actual transactions, a bank can examine transaction patterns on encrypted data to spot questionable activity.

- **Secure Data Sharing**

  For joint initiatives, organizations frequently need to exchange data while keeping it private. By enabling parties to do computations on shared encrypted data without disclosing their datasets, homomorphic encryption makes this possible. Example: Without disclosing their client information, two businesses can collaborate on analytics of sales data.

- **Machine Learning**

  Large volumes of data are needed for both training and inference in machine learning algorithms. Sensitive information may be used for model training while maintaining privacy thanks to homomorphic encryption. For instance, a business may use encrypted client data to train its AI model, guaranteeing that private information is kept private at all times.

Benefits of Homomorphic Encryption for Secure Data Processing

There are several strong arguments in favour of homomorphic encryption for safe data processing, including:

- **Enhanced Security**

  Increased security is the main benefit of homomorphic encryption. Businesses may greatly lower the risk of data breaches by encrypting data while it is being processed. A hostile actor will only come across ciphertext and not the sensitive underlying data, even if they manage to access the computer environment.

- **Privacy Preservation**

  In a time when worries about data privacy are growing, homomorphic encryption offers a way to protect privacy while allowing for data analysis. People can keep their data under control and stop illegal access.

- **Compliance with Regulations**

  Strict guidelines on how businesses handle personal data are enforced by data protection laws like the General Data Protection Regulation (GDPR) and the Health Insurance Portability and Accountability Act (HIPAA). Because homomorphic encryption makes it possible to process sensitive data securely, it can help organizations adhere to these rules.

- **Enabling Collaboration**

  Organizations may collaborate securely thanks to homomorphic encryption. By working on common projects together without disclosing private information, parties can promote cooperation and confidence.

Practical Challenges of Homomorphic Encryption

Despite its potential, homomorphic encryption is not widely used due to a number of real-world issues. These are the biggest obstacles:

Performance and Efficiency

Performance is one of the main issues with homomorphic encryption. Compared to conventional techniques, the computational cost of operating with encrypted data is much greater. Slower processing times and higher latency might result from this inefficiency.

- **Comparison**: Depending on the complexity of the calculation, simple operations on plaintext could take microseconds, whereas operations on encrypted data could take seconds or even longer.

Complexity of Implementation

Homomorphic encryption can be difficult to implement and calls for certain expertise. The HE libraries and algorithms are still developing, making it difficult to integrate them into current systems.

- **Barriers to Adoption**: The apparent complexity of HE and the requirement for qualified staff to install and manage the system may make organizations reluctant to embrace it.

Limited Functionality

Although FHE permits arbitrary calculations, the actual applications sometimes restrict the complexity of the functions that may be computed or call for particular kinds of operations. Some schemes could require extra modifications since they don't natively support specific mathematical functions.

- **Operational Constraints**: This restriction could affect how well HE works in some situations when intricate processes are necessary.

Noise Management

Every operation on encrypted data adds noise, which might build up and prevent the decryption of the ciphertext. Controlling this noise is essential because it restricts how many operations can be carried out before the data must be refreshed or re-encrypted.

- **Impact on Usability**: Implementing and using homomorphic encryption operationally can be made more difficult by noise control, especially in settings where calculations must be performed often.

Future of Homomorphic Encryption

Homomorphic encryption has a bright future since research is still being done to overcome its obstacles. The effectiveness and usefulness of HE are anticipated to increase with advancements in hardware acceleration, optimization strategies, and algorithm design.

Trends to Watch

- **Performance Enhancements**: Methods to lower the computational overhead of HE are being investigated by researchers. Faster calculations on encrypted data might result from improvements in cryptography primitives and optimized algorithms.

- **Broader Adoption**: Secure data processing solutions like homomorphic encryption are expected to become more and more in demand as businesses become more conscious of data privacy issues and legal constraints.

- **Integration with Emerging Technologies**: Combining HE with other cutting-edge technologies like blockchain and artificial intelligence may open up new use cases and applications (Bhuyan, 2017).

5.6 AI-Driven Insider Threat Detection

Insider threats are cybersecurity dangers that come from within a company and usually include workers, subcontractors, or other reliable people who have access to networks, systems, or private information. These risks can be purposeful, as when an employee steals private data on purpose, or inadvertent, such when a well-meaning insider unintentionally reveals important assets due to carelessness, human error, or inadequate security procedures (Zscaler, 2024).

Threat detection and response is enterprise cybersecurity in a nutshell – it's the all-encompassing term for the processes and technologies that go into identifying potential security threats. The wide range of attacks and techniques that need to be caught include malware, Unauthorized access, data breaches, or any other actions that can jeopardize an organization's information systems' availability, confidentiality, or integrity.

Not only is it the <u>Security Operations Centre's responsibility to keep all of the above in check</u>, but the goal is to detect these threats as early as possible to minimize damage. This is a tall order; especially when relying on purely human teams. This article will break down threat detection and response into its components, and see where AI-driven threat detection is poised to make the biggest changes (Nedunoori, 2024).

Types of Insider Threats

Insider threats can take many different forms, and each one presents different security posture concerns for an organisation. These attacks are particularly harmful in today's hyperconnected environments where connection and trusted access might unintentionally increase dangers since they can circumvent conventional defences like firewalls or take advantage of flaws in VPN installations.

- **Malicious Insider Threats**

  Malicious insiders are those who purposefully jeopardize security within a company for their own benefit or out of animosity. A typical example would be a dissatisfied employee selling access credentials to hackers or stealing intellectual property. Because they are frequently driven by monetary rewards, emotional grudges, or a desire for vengeance, these threats are especially challenging to identify.

  If appropriate security measures aren't in place, insiders can readily take advantage of their already legitimate access to critical data. Strict access control, ongoing monitoring, and behavioral analytics are necessary to stop malevolent insider threats before they cause harm.

  Example: One of the best-known instances of a malevolent insider is Edward Snowden, a former NSA contractor. Snowden released sensitive material regarding the NSA's and its allies' worldwide monitoring initiatives. Although his activities were motivated more by ideology than by money, they nonetheless demonstrate the harm that one insider may cause.

- **Accidental Insider Threats**

  Accidental insider risks happen when workers unintentionally allow cyberattacks to happen. Examples that occur often include falling for phishing schemes, adjusting security settings incorrectly, or inadvertently disclosing private information to unapproved parties. One of the most frequent sources of insider threats is human mistake, which emphasizes why depending only on perimeter defences is no longer adequate.

Organizations must put in place ongoing training and awareness initiatives to counteract unintentional insider risks.

Example: In 2017, an employee unintentionally misplaced a USB device that had private security information about Heathrow Airport's operations. A member of the public found the disc, which contained facts about the Queen's travel itinerary, patrol schedules, and security procedures. Although there was thankfully no large breach, the episode demonstrated how unintentional insider activities, such as misplacing sensitive data, can result in serious security problems.

- **Negligent Insider Threats**

  Employees that disregard security best practices out of negligence or ignorance are known as negligent insiders. This might be as easy as using unapproved devices, exchanging passwords, or disregarding fundamental security procedures. Although not malevolent, these actions leave significant gaps that hackers may take advantage of.

  In order to reduce the dangers presented by careless insiders, businesses must implement stringent security procedures and hold staff members responsible for adhering to them.

  Example: An employee of Facebook stored unencrypted payroll data on their personal laptop in 2020, which was against company policy. Regretfully, the laptop was taken, exposing private data belonging to almost 29,000 workers. Even though there was no proof that the data was being exploited, this careless act of managing private data improperly may have had fatal repercussions.

- **Third-Party Insider Threats**

  Third-party insider risks originate from partners, contractors, or suppliers who have access to the data or systems of an organization. These outside partners bring more risk factors even if they are necessary for operations. In the event that a contractor's credentials are stolen or a third-party system is penetrated, attackers may get critical data, sometimes without detection.

Example: The Home Depot data breach happened as a result of hackers using credentials that were obtained from a third-party vendor to access the company's systems. 56 million credit card details were exposed in this hack, which emphasizes the dangers third parties provide when appropriate access restrictions aren't in place.

In order to manage these risks, third-party users must be given the bare minimum of access and be closely watched when interacting with internal systems. This is done by applying the least-privilege concept. This risk may be considerably decreased by implementing stringent access restrictions and routine security evaluations of third-party partners (Zscaler, 2024).

Implementing AI in Threat Detection Systems

A careful strategy is necessary to ensure a smooth integration of AI in threat detection with your company's current security architecture. Let's examine some of the most important factors to take into account while putting AI threat detection into practice.

- **Integration with Existing Security Infrastructure**

  Adding AI to your threat detection system is not a simple solution. You should be aware that artificial intelligence (AI) systems need to work seamlessly with an organization's current security solutions, including firewalls, intrusion detection/prevention systems (IDS/IPS), and security information and event management (SIEM) systems.

  Artificial intelligence (AI) technologies enhance current systems by adding sophisticated threat detection and predictive analytics, not dispensing with them. The majority of AI systems have connectors or APIs to facilitate simple integration with the current infrastructure.

- **Real-Time Monitoring and Alerts**

  One of AI's primary skills for threat detection is real-time network, system, and user behaviour monitoring. AI systems are able to continually check the data for irregularities. This makes it possible to identify such hazards early on before they have a chance to do serious harm. Furthermore, real-time notifications can be produced by threat detection systems driven by AI. This makes it possible for security personnel to be informed of security issues right away and react quickly to reduce risks.

- **Automation of Responses**

  Through reaction action automation, AI may improve threat detection systems. AI can, for instance, automatically initiate certain pre-established security procedures once a danger has been identified. It may also be used to reset compromised user passwords or block suspicious IP addresses. The time between detection and reaction is greatly shortened by this automation, which also lessens the possibility of cyberattack harm.

- **Scalability and Flexibility**

  The tremendous scalability of AI-based threat detection systems makes them appropriate for a wide range of organizations. Artificial Intelligence-based threat detection systems are increasingly indispensable as cyber threats continue to evolve and increase in volume. These systems are capable of handling massive volumes of data without compromising efficiency. Additionally, organizations may tailor detection settings and actions to meet their unique needs thanks to the flexibility that AI systems offer(SentinelOne, 2024a).

5.7 Developments in Edge Computing Security for Cloud Databases

Cloud computing, which provides scalable and effective computing power, storage, and applications via the internet, has become a key component in the changing landscape of digital transformation. This paradigm change has made it possible for companies to take use of enormous resources without requiring a large amount of physical infrastructure, which has improved flexibility and reduced costs. Because Cloud computing is centralized, data and computational resources may be consolidated to provide dependable and strong services that are accessible from anywhere in the world.

In order to bridge the gap between data creation and data processing, edge computing emerged as an appealing addition to the Cloud. Whether it be IoT devices, mobile phones, or local edge servers, edge computing greatly lowers latency, saves bandwidth, and speeds up reaction times by processing data closer to the point of generation. By addressing applications that need to analyze and make decisions in real time, this decentralized method expands Cloud computing's capabilities to the network's edge.

Businesses looking to embrace digital innovation and streamline operations must comprehend the connection between edge and Cloud computing. This mutually beneficial partnership promotes scalability, increases efficiency, and guarantees that applications may take advantage of the special advantages of both paradigms. As we examine this link in further detail, it becomes evident that integrating edge and Cloud computing is not only a technological achievement but also a strategic requirement for companies operating in the digital era.

Exploring Edge Computing

Definition and Key Features

Edge computing is a distributed computing paradigm that shifts processing and data storage closer to the point of demand in order to improve response times and save bandwidth. Among its main features are localized data processing, less reliance on a centralized Cloud, and the ability to perform effectively in situations with limited connection or remote locations. This approach reduces the gap between data sources and processing power while facilitating real-time data analysis and decision-making.

Advantages of Edge Computing

- **Reduced Latency:** Edge computing significantly lowers latency or the time it takes for data transmission to start after an order to do so, by processing data close to its source. This is essential for applications like online gaming, real-time analytics, and driverless cars that need to process and act instantly.

- **Bandwidth Savings:** Significant bandwidth savings are achieved by edge computing, which eliminates the need to transport enormous volumes of data across the network to a central Cloud. When network connectivity is costly or scarce, this efficiency is especially advantageous.

Enhanced Privacy and Security

Edge computing's built-in local data processing can improve security and privacy because private data doesn't need to travel across the internet to get to a central server. More regulated data access is made possible by this localized strategy, which also lessens the attack surface for online threats(Lee, 2024).

- **Clouds database**

  According to certain study estimates, Cloud database storage is expected to rise by more than 60% annually through 2018. This is a time of significant expansion for the technology industry. Unquestionably, the potential to keep databases online for easy access by many departments and user types is alluring; nevertheless, as with other forms of Cloud computing, there is some danger associated with server database storage. As more businesses migrate their databases online, network security teams may better prepare for intrusion attempts and lessen the impact of successful breaches by being aware of the hazards associated with

Cloud computing. This article describes ways to lower security risks and identifies some of the vulnerabilities to Cloud database systems.

Possible Threat Types

Threats to Cloud database systems are similar to those that impact Cloud technology. However, because to the nature of databases containing vast volumes of potentially sensitive data, the consequences can be serious if left unchecked. These hazards provide an idea of the kinds of risks that network managers face when businesses use extensive Cloud database storage systems, even if they are not an exhaustive list.

- **Data breaches** – According to media reports, data breaches are arguably the most frequent hazard to Cloud databases. In a data breach, hackers get private data that is kept on Cloud servers, including postal addresses or credit card details, and utilize it for their own benefit. Data breaches might become more serious as more information is kept online in one place, possibly impacting millions of clients or staff at once.

- **Account hijacking** – Hackers attempt to access a user's account by phishing or by finding passwords through flaws in software security measures. After stealing a user's login credentials, hackers typically alter the password to prevent users from accessing their accounts. At this stage, the user has unrestricted access to any files or other material kept in their Cloud, including database data that may include information on several users simultaneously.

- **APIs** – The technological method by which a user interacts with a Cloud system and determines what rights they have to connect third-party apps to the system is called an Application Programming Interface (API). Even while Cloud storage providers and other online organizations have made significant progress in creating safe APIs, such OAuth, there is always a chance that a hacker would discover flaws to access administrator API areas.

- **Data loss** – One potential consequence of an intruder gaining access to private data is that the data may be erased to cause the owner trouble. If users fail to maintain current backups of their files, they may be tampered with and lost forever. When every file is kept on a single Cloud-based server, deletions may spread to every user device, erasing all of the files at once.

- **Cloud servers as malware platforms** – Database files may be kept current across platforms and devices with the use of Cloud computing's synchronizing services. But what if an attacker chooses to make advantage of the same synchronization method to spread malware to every user device at once? Attackers may cause significantly more harm if they could use Cloud servers to propagate malware throughout a network than if they could simply impact a small, locally stored organization's network (University, 2024).

5.8 Chapter Summary

Cloud database security is a growing and constantly developing field due to novel technologies that adapt to new threats and challenges. Federated learning has appeared as innovative, the approach that lets train a model across multiple devices without sharing the data, which is extremely significant in such industries as healthcare or finance. Multi-Cloud security solutions improve control and protection of various Cloud ecosystems through utilizing artificial intelligence manifested in the capacity to identify security threats and respond to them automatically as well as enforcing consistent security policies. Blockchain technology is emerging as a key enabler of Cloud security through decentralized, immutable records that can enable secure Cloud exchange, audit, and agility through smart contracts. However, developments in homomorphic encryption introduce a revolution in secure data sharing, enabling computation with encrypted data without data decryption to protect data integrity in areas that may be shared or multi-user.

The adoption of AI-based threat detection systems that utilize machine learning algorithms to find patterns in user activity and identify potentially dangerous trends or spikes that may be halted before they because serious harm is crucial since the insider threat problem is still extremely serious. As with these upgrades, improvements in edge computing security are also witnessed, primarily in how to guard Cloud databases that are incorporated in a decentralized structure. These are zero-trust architectures, data synchronization with security protocols, and efficient lightweight encryption for constrained edge devices. In this regard, they address risks triggered by distributed data processing and boost real-time decision-making. These key developments are examined in this chapter in order to capture their implications in terms of the kinds of security paradigms that may be possible for Cloud databases. With the practical application of federated learning, blockchain AI, and enhanced security measures, security strategies that are intelligent, scalable, and robust can be adapted to deliver security in today's Cloud services. These advancements taken altogether enable businesses to protect data and meet compliance requirements while enhancing confidence in the Cloud environments to meet the call of digital transformation.

Multiple-choice questions (MCQs)

1. **What is federated learning, and how does it contribute to secure data processing?**

    a. A centralized approach for processing all data in a single location

    b. A decentralized method that allows models to be trained locally on data, improving privacy and security

    c. A method of encrypting all data before processing

    d. A data-sharing technique that involves moving data to a central server

2. **How do AI-powered multi-cloud security solutions enhance cloud database security?**

   a. By managing resources in a single cloud provider

   b. By enabling the simultaneous monitoring and protection of data across multiple cloud platforms using AI-based threat detection

   c. By encrypting all data in transit

   d. By reducing the cost of cloud storage

3. **What role does blockchain play in enhancing cloud security?**

   a. It stores all cloud database data in decentralized ledgers

   b. It provides a transparent and tamper-proof mechanism for securing data transactions and enhancing access control

   c. It speeds up the cloud service provider's network

   d. It increases the computational resources of cloud servers

4. **What is homomorphic encryption, and how does it secure data sharing?**

   a. It encrypts data only when it is stored in the cloud

   b. It enables computations to be performed on encrypted data without needing to decrypt it first, ensuring privacy during data sharing

   c. It uses a central authority to monitor all data access

   d. It encrypts data in transit only

5. **How does AI-driven insider threat detection work in cloud database security?**

   a. It analyzes patterns of behavior and identifies deviations from normal activities that may indicate insider threats

   b. It prevents external cyber-attacks using firewalls

   c. It focuses only on preventing data breaches from outside sources

   d. It encrypts all user communications in the cloud

6. **What is the role of edge computing in cloud database security?**

    a. It centralizes all security functions in a data center

    b. It processes data closer to the source (at the "edge"), reducing latency and improving real-time security by handling data locally

    c. It reduces the need for encryption

    d. It focuses only on hardware security

7. **What is a primary benefit of federated learning in cloud database security?**

    a. It requires centralized data storage

    b. It allows for machine learning models to be trained on distributed data without transferring sensitive data, enhancing privacy

    c. It prevents all types of cloud attacks

    d. It eliminates the need for cloud encryption

8. **How do AI-powered multi-cloud security solutions address the complexity of managing data across different cloud platforms?**

    a. By focusing on securing a single cloud provider

    b. By using AI to automate threat detection and response across various cloud environments, ensuring comprehensive protection

    c. By reducing the number of cloud services used

    d. By relying on manual monitoring and response

9. **Why is homomorphic encryption considering a key technology for secure data sharing in the cloud?**

    a. It allows data to remain encrypted during computation, ensuring that no sensitive data is exposed during analysis or processing

    b. It stores data in a single encrypted server

    c. It reduces data storage costs in the cloud

    d. It increases the speed of data access

10. **What development in edge computing contributes to enhanced cloud database security?**

    a. Storing more data at the cloud server

    b. Performing real-time data analysis and threat detection at the edge of the network, reducing risks associated with latency and centralized data processing

    c. Encrypting data during cloud transfers

    d. Using blockchain to manage local storage security

Answers

1	2	3	4	5	6	7	8	9	10
B	B	B	B	A	B	B	B	A	B

Chapter 06

FUTURE TRENDS AND CHALLENGES IN CLOUD DATABASE SECURITY

6.1 Chapter Overview

The development of new technologies, security risks, and artificial intelligence in Cloud systems are examined and discussed in chapter 6 of the next chapter, Future Trends and Challenges in Cloud Database Security. The chapter introduces the complexity of Cloud database environments and the issues that arise with the implementation of multi-cloud and hybrid systems. It then progresses to give a briefing to the evolving security, calling for points of advanced attacks like ransomware, phishing, and SQL injection on Cloud databases.

It also emphasizes potential and threats that quantum computing poses to conventional cryptography in the era of Cloud security. It also discusses privacy-preserving method in machine learning, especially the method that ensures that the raw data does not leak in the learning process; the two methods described here include differential privacy and homomorphic encryption. There is one more practice area to explore about AI security legal and ethical aspects: Liability, data privacy protection, and the need to develop an ethical approach to AI. Last but not least, it calculates the Cloud database security regulations and compliance and at last brings light on the interaction of hybrid AI & integrated Cloud security systems to resolve the problem of modern-day's Cloud structure.

6.2 The Growing Complexity of Cloud Database Environments

The term "Cloud complexity" describes the complexities and difficulties that come up during the planning, implementation, administration, and use of Cloud computing systems. It includes the several levels, parts, and connections that make up a Cloud infrastructure, which can get more complicated when businesses use and combine more than one Cloud service, platform, and provider.

Cloud computing may streamline, unify, and scale resources more efficiently, which can simplify many organizational operations. However, it also brings additional complications that might be difficult for companies that lack sufficient Cloud knowledge. Attempting to resolve these difficulties is a widespread issue; according to a recent Hitachi research that polled IT leaders, 45% of companies had trouble "navigating complex Cloud landscapes".

8 Common Cloud Complexity Causes

Cloud complexity may be caused by both technological and organizational issues, but the underlying causes can vary depending on how the environment is configured and what a business wants to achieve.

In general, some of things can contribute to Cloud complexity, like as:

Eight Causes of Cloud Complexity

Sources: - *(Tierpoint, 2024)*

- **Multi-cloud and Hybrid Cloud Environments:** Businesses frequently use a combination of private, public, and hybrid Cloud solutions, which may make things more complicated because of the requirement for data synchronization, platform management, and interoperability.

- **Data Gravity:** An organization's data collection grows significantly every day. The intricacy of maintaining and transferring data between Cloud systems can increase with data quantities, particularly when working with big datasets or real-time data processing.

- **Security and Compliance:** The shared responsibility model between Cloud providers and clients, together with the necessity to safeguard data across numerous environments, can make it difficult to ensure the security of data and apps in the Cloud and to comply with compliance standards.

- **Application and Infrastructure Interdependencies:** Because Cloud systems can entail intricate interdependencies between infrastructure, services, and applications, it can be challenging to comprehend and control the effects of changes or failures.

- **Integration Challenges:** Complexities like as data transfer, API compatibility, and guaranteeing smooth communication between on-premises and Cloud-based apps might arise when integrating current legacy systems with Cloud settings.

- **Skills and Expertise:** Organisations may find it difficult to recruit and keep the specialized skills and experience needed to manage Cloud complexity internally. Overcoming the learning curve required to comprehend the variety of services offered, establish interoperability across several frameworks, and safeguard data in one or more Cloud environments may also be difficult.

- **Cost Management:** Cost management in Cloud systems may become more complicated, particularly when demand fluctuates. To prevent unforeseen costs, organizations must estimate future demands, analyze consumption trends, and allocate resources as efficiently as possible.

- **Other Organizational Issues:** Uncertain regulations and processes regarding Cloud use, as well as overcoming opposition from some workers who might be less inclined to use the Cloud, might potentially provide difficulties.

Cloud Complexity is a Concern for Organizations

Cloud complexity is more than simply a theoretical problem; it has practical ramifications for companies trying to integrate the Cloud into more of their operations. The impact of Cloud complexity, including repercussions that contradict the promised advantages of Cloud computing, must be taken into account by organizations wishing to use the Cloud for digital transformation initiatives.

- **Cloud Complexity is a Concern for Organizations:** Cloud complexity has practical ramifications for companies aiming to integrate the Cloud into more of their operations; it is not only a theoretical problem. Businesses wishing to use the Cloud for digital transformation initiatives need to think about the complexity of the Cloud, including negative effects that might offset any possible advantages of Cloud computing.

Why is Cloud Complexity a Concern?

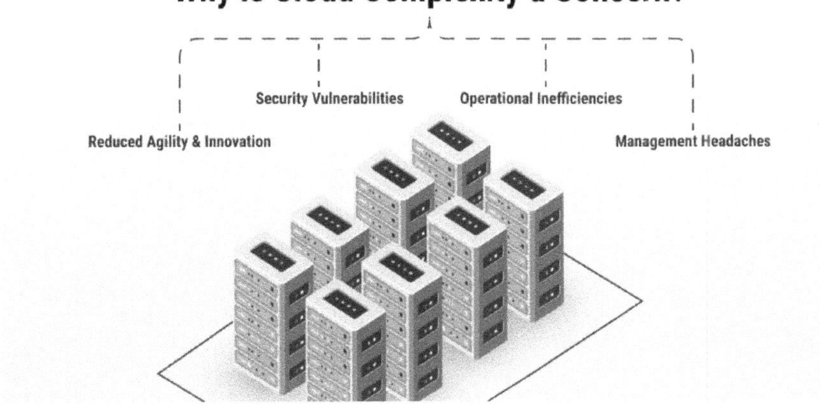

Sources: - *(Tierpoint, 2024)*

1. **Reduced Agility and Innovation:** BIncreased agility and innovative potential are two major advantages for businesses that adopt the Cloud. But if Cloud complexity is not effectively managed, it may also impede innovation and decrease agility. Overseeing complex settings with unique web interfaces and security protocols might divert attention from important innovation projects.

2. **Security Vulnerabilities:** Every layer added to an IT environment can generate a new list of security vulnerabilities and concerns. According to IBM's 2023 Cost of a Data Breach report, companies with more complex security systems experienced higher costs associated with data breaches, averaging $5.28 million, compared to businesses with low or no complexity in their security systems at $3.84 million. IT leaders need to identify every touchpoint and potential door attackers may take to infiltrate their systems, which becomes more difficult as Cloud environments get more complex.

3. **Operational Inefficiencies:** Even while provisioning, patching, and troubleshooting are straightforward procedures, they may rapidly become wasteful when carried out across several Cloud environments or in a hybrid Cloud system that incorporates on-

premises frameworks. If the difficulties are not resolved, it may be tempting to go back to on-premises IT as the jobs seem easier there.

4. **Management Headaches:** Cloud complexity may turn managers from proactive to reactive by creating an endless to-do list if it is not handled. This can produce employee fatigue that affects the team at all levels, impede other, more crucial strategic activities, and lead to frustration. These difficulties make controlling Cloud complexity essential.

What is Multi-Cloud?

Multi-Cloud strategies come into play when organizations leverage a blend of private and public Cloud providers like Azure, AWS, and Google Cloud in their IT infrastructure. Previously, the focus was on Cloud migration and vendor selection.

Today, the shift is towards harnessing solutions from multiple Cloud vendors. As Cloud adoption matures, core functionalities among major players become increasingly similar. However, each vendor offers unique services with variations in delivery.

Considerations include Kubernetes cluster provisioning time, low-latency network availability, storage costs across performance tiers, and Identity and Access Management (IAM) service compatibility. Multi-Cloud solutions provide flexibility in selecting desired services, but with inherent complexities.

Here are five key considerations before opting for the multi-cloud model:

- **Cost-Saving Awareness:** Ensure your business understands potential cost-saving aspects of navigating multi-cloud complexity.

- **Clarity and Reliability:** Invest in tooling to maintain clarity and reliability within the multi-cloud environment.

- **Cloud Exploration:** Begin exploring multiple Cloud environments to grasp similarities and differences in the context of multi-cloud complexity.

- **Savings Evaluation:** Always evaluate areas with the potential for significant savings within the multi-cloud framework.

- **Automation Emphasis:** Continuously strive to automate processes to manage the increasing complexity inherent in multi-cloud environments.

Let's explore some examples to illustrate these nuances and shed light on the intricacies of multi-cloud complexity (Squadcast, 2024).

6.3 Emerging Security Threats and Attack Vectors

In cyber security, understanding attack routes is essential to protecting data and systems. The method by which hackers exploit flaws in a network, system, or application is known as an attack vector. The term "attack vectors" describes the several ways that hackers might enter a system, network, or application without authorization in order to take advantage of security holes, steal information, or do harm.

It's more crucial than ever to recognize and defend against these attack vectors as cyber-attacks become more sophisticated. The many attack vector types, their impact on cybersecurity, and countermeasures will all be covered in this article.

What is Attack Vectors?

The particular routes or techniques that cybercriminals employ to obtain unauthorized access to a system, network, or application are known as attack vectors. By acting as entrance sites for assaults, these vectors enable malevolent actors to take advantage of weaknesses. Each ethical hacker uses a different attack method to determine whether the target application—which may be an Android or web application—is secure.

They use the system's vulnerabilities to steal data, inflict harm, or seize control.

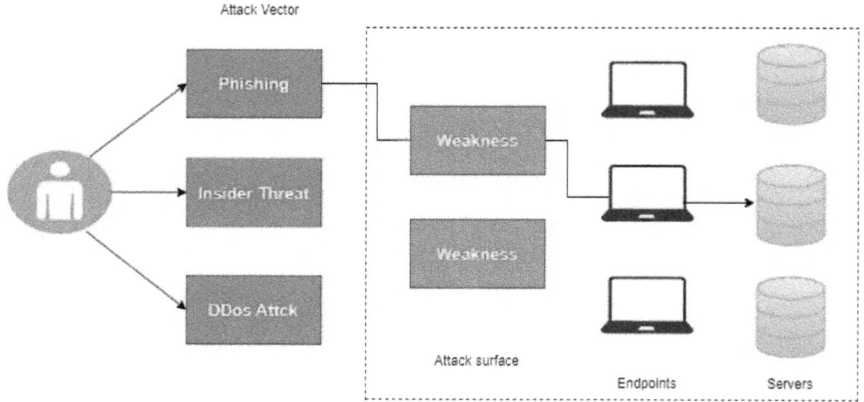

Source:- *(geeksforgreeks, 2024)*

Some Common Attack Vectors in Cybersecurity

- **Phishing:** A cyberattack of this kind involves tricking a victim or user into clicking on malicious websites that are designed to look real. The most popular method of phishing is sending spam emails that look real in order to deprive the target of all their credentials.

- **Malware:** Any program intended to damage computer systems, networks, or users is referred to as malware, short for malicious software. Malware is made to access computer systems without the user's consent, usually for the advantage of a third party.

- **MITM:** An undesired proxy in the network intercepts and alters requests and answers in Man-in-the-Middle (MitM) attacks. We refer to this proxy as a "man in the middle."

- **Denial of Service**: A denial-of-service (DoS) attack is a cyberattack on a single computer or website that aims to interfere with an organization's network operations by preventing its users from accessing it. In an effort to overload systems and stop some or all valid requests from being completed, it is accomplished by bombarding the targeted machine or resource with excessive requests.

- **Insider Attacks**: Insiders who have previously had access to sensitive information, such as former workers, business partners, contractors, or security administrators, are the source of insider threats or attacks.

- **Ransomware**: Ransomware is a type of malicious software that encrypts data and keeps people from accessing it.

- **SQL Injection:** SQL injection is a code injection method that allows an attacker to insert malicious SQL commands into web page inputs and obtain unauthorized access to a database.

Recent Cyber Security Attacks

- **Infosys**: A data breach that affected Infosys McCamish Systems, the US division of the Indian IT services business Infosys, occurred in November 2023. The organization is now looking into the implications of the intrusion, which caused many applications to go unavailable.

- **Indian Council of Medical Research**: In October 2023, a data breach compromised the health information of over 815 million Indian residents. A threat actor known as "pwn0001" was responsible for the breach and claimed to have the data for sale.

- **Hyundai Motor Europe**: The assailants of the Black Basta ransomware assault, which targeted Hyundai Motor Europe in February 2024, claim to have taken 3TB of company data.

- **Boeing**: In November 2024, Boeing disclosed a cyberattack that affected many areas of their operations. Lock Bit, the ransomware group that attacked it, first claimed blame, but Boeing affirmed that the incident had no impact on flight safety.

Ways to Protect Your Organization from Attack Vectors

- **Network Segmentation**: The practice of splitting a computer network into smaller, isolated sections or subnetworks is known as network segmentation. Network isolation or network segregation are other terms that are occasionally used interchangeably with network segmentation. where network hardware like routers, switches, or firewalls divide one segment from the others.

- **Intrusion Detection and Prevention System:** An intrusion detection and prevention system is another name for an intrusion prevention system. It is an application for network security that keeps an eye out for dangerous behaviour on systems or networks. Intrusion prevention systems' primary duties include spotting harmful behaviour, gathering data about it, reporting it, and making an effort to block or halt it.

- **Antivirus:** Anti-Malware/Antivirus One kind of software application that aids in defending the computer system from malware and viruses is called software. It finds and eliminates viruses from the computer system. Additionally, it shields the computer system from some types of viruses.

- **Encryption**: Data encryption is a technique used to protect the secrecy of data by converting it into ciphertext that can only be decrypted using a special decryption key generated either before or during the encryption process. Encryption is the process by which plaintext is transformed into ciphertext.

What is an Attack Surface?

Every place, interface, or channel that an attacker may use to gain unauthorized access to a system, network, or application is referred to as an attack surface. It includes all of the weaknesses, entry points, and possible avenues of attack that are present inside the cyberspace of an organization (geeksforgreeks, 2024).

6.4 The Role of Quantum Computing in Cloud Security

The continual expansion and interconnections of the digital world have made cybersecurity an increasingly critical concern for everyone from individuals to corporations to nation-states. The arrival of quantum computing, however, is poised to radically alter today's cybersecurity landscape. This detailed guide goes into quantum computing's crucial impact on, and contradiction to, cybersecurity, stretching to include the implications, as well as the preventive measures to make cyberspace a secure field.

What is Quantum Computing?

Superposition and entanglement are two quantum-mechanical phenomena that are used in quantum computing to manipulate data in ways that are not possible with binary systems like the standard conventional computer. Bits, the smallest units of data, are used in traditional computers and are denoted by the numbers 0 and 1. Qubits, another name for quantum bits, are used in quantum computers. The basic characteristics of qubits are superposition and entanglement, which allow one qubit to represent many states at once. This indicates that quantum computers can handle a wide range of cybersecurity possibilities and threats, as well as challenges that are far too complex to handle at a very quick speed.

Impact of Quantum Computing on Cryptography

The foundation for modern cybersecurity is cryptography, which encrypts sensitive data to keep it safe. Because of the digital world's ongoing growth and interconnections, cybersecurity is becoming a crucial issue for everyone, including individuals, businesses, and nation-states. But the advancements of quantum computing have the potential to change the state of cybersecurity as it exists today. Because of the digital world's ongoing growth and interconnections, cybersecurity is becoming a crucial issue for everyone, including individuals, businesses, and nation-states.

Preparing for the Quantum Threat: Post-Quantum Cryptography

Going Quantum-Resistant: Post-Quantum Cryptography means algorithms that are quantum safe. Companies should support post-quantum, quantum-resistant algorithms, as none of their encryption procedures currently employ them. To combat the threat

posed by quantum computing, academics from all across the world are developing post-quantum encryption techniques. These algorithms allow businesses to continue preserving their essential data since they are resistant to attacks from both conventional and quantum computers. Roadblocks and Transition to Post-Quantum Cryptographic System Deployment.

Building quantum-safe systems through existing cryptographic libraries is a critical investment in preparation for the post-quantum threat. Much effort is underway to approach and standardize quantum-resistant cryptographic algorithms that are recommended in real-world web security environments. Cryptographic libraries, for example, which implement the NIST (sell) cryptography suite across operating platforms support commercial interests to maximize internet reliability. Though the end of public-key cryptography is not upon us, the use of a mechanism that provides quantum-safe encryption appears necessary in a world that will increasingly be controlled by quantum computers armed with Shor's algorithm. This Does not imply it will be done. Currently, the National Institute of Standards and Technology (NIST) is spearheading an initiative aimed at standardizing post-quantum encryption.

Quantum Key Distribution: Secure Communication Revolution

One of the main applications of quantum mechanics in cybersecurity is quantum key distribution (QKD), an unparalleled method of providing safe key transmission for end users. It uses entanglement and superposition to identify an eavesdropper interfering with a key exchange and notify the communication parties of the intruder's presence. The method is practically guaranteed to function in practice. BB84 is one of the to start with to begin with well-known Traditions for QKD, created by Charles Bennett and Gilles Brassard in 1984. Additionally, QKD has been finding pragmatic applications, as different organizations and governments have started creating a quantum-protected communication network for the purpose of securing data that must remain secret.

Enhanced Security Protocols and Key Achievements Achieved Through Quantum Computing

Quantum computing has a game-changing influence on the security solutions that are currently in place as it has the potential to strengthen existing protocols or dismantle them. Quantum algorithms can improve network security, intrusion detection systems, and authentication systems. For instance, Grover (1996) found a method for locating items faster in a database compared to an unsorted database's traditional search. This phenomenon can be used to find large data sets Fast and identify security vulnerabilities – that is, strengthening the overall security infrastructure.

Quantum Cybersecurity Problems and Considerations

Quantum computing poses significant difficulties, despite its potential. Creating and maintaining quantum computers is both costly and complex, and it will be some time before we see big (fault-tolerant) quantum computers anywhere. Furthermore, transitioning to cryptographic systems immune to quantum threats requires coordinated effort between industries and governments. From an ethical and legal standpoint, there are other factors to consider, as well. The potential for misuse exists as the technology is very powerful. To make sure quantum computing benefits humanity, people from around the world should work together in partnership with an effective regulatory system. Policymakers need to understand these problems to avoid exacerbating existing security problems and make sure quantum advances work for everyone's benefit.

Challenges and Considerations

While the plausible advantages of quantum computing in Cloud offerings are immense, there are several challenges and issues to address:

1. **Technological Maturity:** The field of quantum computing remains young. Effective, large-scale quantum computing may yet be years or possibly many years away because building scalable and impermeable quantum computer systems is extremely difficult. Cloud carriers will prefer to spend on lookup and improvement to integrate quantum computing expertise efficiently.

2. **Infrastructure Requirements:** Quantum computer structures want precise infrastructure with extremely low temperatures and distant locations to maintain qubit coherence. This infrastructure's development and maintenance are high-priced and complicated. In addition to sacrificing reliability and performance, organizations providing Cloud services will look to combine quantum computing with their existing infrastructure.

3. **Talent and Expertise:** There is currently a dearth of knowledge and specialized expertise in quantum computing. Cloud provider vendors will want to invest in training and employing quantum computing experts to design, manage, and optimize quantum-powered Cloud services.

4. **Data Security and Privacy:** Although quantum cryptography promises even higher security, the development of quantum computers also puts current encryption techniques at risk. In a post-quantum era, Cloud provider carriers will want to ensure statistical protection by enforcing stricter encryption regulations (shashank, 2024).

6.5 Privacy-Preserving Machine Learning Techniques

Massive data collection is a key component of Artificial Intelligence (AI) methodologies, and ML, the core component of AI, leverages this data to build predictive models. However, there is a difference between gathering data and using it to identify patterns in its behaviour. Furthermore, there are a number of challenges that someone or an organization must overcome, including privacy issues like data breaches, monetary loss, and damage to one's reputation.

"Machine learning powers a large portion of the most privacy-sensitive data analysis, which primarily consists of search algorithms, recommender systems, and AdTech networks."(Cameron F. Kerry, 2020)

The objective of privacy-preserving machine learning is to combine the advantages of machine learning with privacy protection. Adhering to data privacy rules and privatizing obtained data are made possible by it. In this article, the fundamental concepts of privacy-preserving machine learning are presented. In order to overcome issues, this article demonstrates how to combine privacy and machine learning techniques. Check out some of of the available tools. This essay seeks to provide readers a thorough grasp of machine learning that protects privacy for a variety of uses.

A methodical technique to stopping data leaking in machine learning algorithms is called Privacy-Preserving Machine Learning. As shown in Figure 1, PPML enables a variety of privacy-enhancing techniques that enable numerous input sources to collaborate on training ML models without disclosing their private information in its original form.

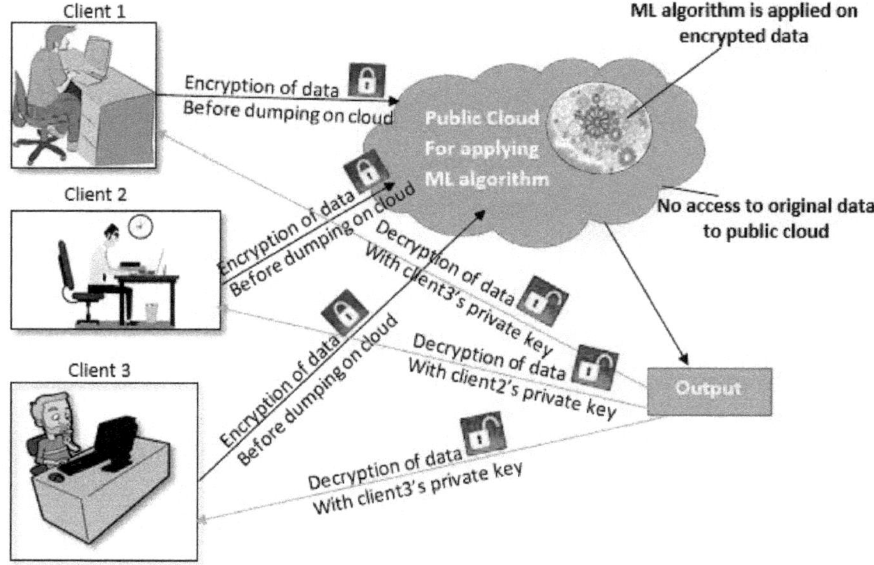

Source: - *(Dulari, 2022)*

Need in Today's Era

Despite the advantages of machine learning applications, there is always a danger to data privacy. Take intrusion detection or healthcare apps, for instance. Data leaks and cyberattacks are become more frequent and costly to respond to. Because they can steal information that can be used to identify individuals or other valuable information that can be sold, cybercriminals are attracted to massive collections of data stored for training purposes. Furthermore, because sensitive data may be retrieved from ML models, the models themselves are vulnerable. For instance, a study report (Shokri et al., 2017) shows how to ascertain whether a record was used in the training dataset for a certain machine learning model. When they tested their approach on machine learning systems from Google Cloud and Amazon, the accuracy rates were 74% and 94%, respectively.

One of the main issues in this context is safeguarding personally identifiable information (PII), or information that can be used to identify a particular person. Companies must adhere to several data protection regulations, including the General Data Protection Regulation (GDPR) in Europe, in addition to protecting PII from potential leaks. The consequences of violating the GDPR might be severe. Cyberattacks risk financial, legal, and reputational repercussions for both the organizations gathering the data and the end users to whom it relates. Simply eliminating personally identifiable information (PII) from a dataset, such names and addresses, would not be enough since other quasi-identifiers may be utilized to identify a particular person inside the collection. For instance, in a research by Latanya Sweeney, Massachusetts Governor William Weld was re-identified using health information that seemed to be anonymized and contained just his ZIP code, gender, and date of birth.(SWEENEY, 2002).

Machine learning aims to tackle these issues by enhancing it with various techniques that safeguard data privacy. These methods include cryptographic techniques like multi-party computing and homomorphic encryption, machine learning-specific techniques like federated learning, and perturbation techniques like differential privacy.

The privacy-preserving machine learning technique was born out of the present Cloud-based situation for machine learning, security of various assets of any organization, and security of data. There won't be a single way to handle all application types using this PPML methodology. Different applications call for different types of privacy care. Additionally, we need to combine the need to create strong, platform-independent procedures with scenario-specific considerations. Despite the recent explosion in research on privacy-preserving machine learning, there is still a disconnect between theory and practical implementations.

Main Four Stakes of Privacy-Preserving

1.   **Data Privacy in Training:** The assurance against the training data being reverse-engineered by a malevolent party. Rebuilding training data and reverse-engineering models is not as hard as one might think,

according to recent research, even though retrieving information about training data and model weights is a little more challenging than retrieving information from plain-text (the technical term for unencrypted) input and output data.

2. **Privacy in Input:** The guarantee that a user's input data won't be seen to anybody else, including the model developer.

3. **Privacy in Output:** The guarantee that only the client whose data is being inferred can access a model's output.

4. **Model Privacy:** The assurance that the model cannot be stolen by an adversary. Many companies provide developers with predictive skills through APIs or, more lately, software that can be downloaded; AI models may be their mainstay. Model privacy, the last of the four stakes to consider, is essential to user and business interests. Businesses won't be as motivated to develop novel products or invest in improving AI capabilities if their rivals may easily copy their models (an act that is not trivial to analyze).

Machine learning models are a major component of many businesses' intellectual property and key products, therefore having one stolen is risky and can have major financial repercussions. Additionally, a model's outputs can be directly stolen or used to reverse-engineer it(Tramèr et al., 2016).

PPML Techniques

These techniques are employed to guarantee that a third party cannot steal the data. Consequently, the following strategies are employed to thwart different attacks:

- **Differential Privacy**

  One kind of privacy that lets you share pertinent details about a dataset without disclosing any personal information about it is called differential privacy. This technique ensures that the outcome of a differentially-private operation cannot be used to associate a particular record with an individual, even if an attacker has access to every entry in a dataset. In other words, the results of the study are not (significantly) affected by the existence of an individual's record in the dataset. Because of this, the privacy risk is essentially the same regardless of whether an individual uses the dataset or not. A number of differentially-private procedures, including the Laplace, exponential, and randomized response techniques, can be used to introduce random noise into the output, so achieving differential privacy.

- **Homomorphic Encryption**

  a. A cryptographic technique called homomorphic encryption (HE) computes encrypted data so that the decrypted output is the same as the output of the original unencrypted input. Here is an illustration of how the method is applied:

  b. A third party who is in charge of finishing a certain computation receives the result after the data owner encrypts it using a homomorphic function;

  c. The result, which is encrypted since the input data is encrypted, is computed by the third party;

  d. After decrypting the output, the data owner obtains the result of the computation performed on the initial plain-text data.

  The third party cannot access the unencrypted input or output during this process.

- **Multi-party Computation**

  A technology called MPC (Multi-Party Computation) enables several users to compute a function without sharing their personal information. The parties are wary of one other and self-contained. Allowing computation on private data while maintaining the privacy of the data is the basic idea. MPC makes certain that every participant gains as much knowledge as possible from the results and their contributions.

Below, we'll discuss many secure MPC techniques. For further details, [25] is an excellent place to start.

Garbled circuits, a cryptographic procedure, are frequently used for two-party secure computation on Boolean functions (circuits). The following are the steps in the protocol:

- The function (circuit) is encrypted (or garbled) by the first party, Alice, and sent to the second party, Bob, together with her encrypted input;

- Bob and Alice use oblivious transfer to encrypt Bob's input, wherein Alice and Bob exchange some data while the sender is not aware of what has been sent;

- Bob obtains the encrypted result after evaluating the function with both encrypted inputs;

Secret sharing is one tactic used in several MPC approaches. The (t, n)-secret sharing mechanism, for instance, allocates a share to each participant after dividing the secret s into n shares. The secret s can be reconstructed when t shares are united, but no information about s is revealed when any t-1 shares are merged. A group of at least t persons can reconstruct the secret, but no group of fewer than t can. This is because the secret is divided.

Although MPC and homomorphic encryption are both efficient privacy techniques, their processing and transmission costs are considerable.

- **Federated Learning**

  Federated learning reduces the risk of data and identity privacy being compromised by enabling decentralized machine learning procedures, which in turn reduces the amount of information exposed from contributor datasets. Federated learning's basic concept is that a central authority's (such as a company's) machine learning (ML) model M can be further trained on new private datasets from data contributors by encouraging each contributor to train locally using their dataset before updating the central model M (i.e., changing the model's parameter).

Specifically, federated learning functions as follows:

1. The central model M is given to a group of n participants (data providers);

2. Every participant generates a new local parameter l by training the model M locally on its own local dataset Zl.

3. Every participant provides an update to the central authority;

4. To update the central model, the central authority creates a new parameter by combining the local parameters of each participant. Until the primary model is thoroughly trained, this process can be repeated.

- **Ensemble Privacy-Preserving Techniques**

  In machine learning, there is no magic bullet for ensuring privacy. These strategies' degree of privacy depends on a number of variables, such as the machine learning algorithm employed, the resources and capabilities of the adversary, and counting. Therefore, it could be required to integrate or put together many privacy-preserving machine learning approaches in order to achieve higher levels of privacy.

Challenges and Future Directions

A number of difficulties and intriguing opportunities for the future arise as privacy-preserving machine learning keeps changing the face of data-driven companies.

Challenges

- **Scalability**: Despite providing exceptional privacy protection, PPML approaches frequently have a computational cost. It's still difficult to guarantee scalability, particularly for large-scale applications. However, for broad adoption, finding the ideal balance between privacy and performance is essential.

- **Regulatory framework**: The data privacy regulatory environment is changing quickly. Strict guidelines for data processing have been established by laws such as the CCPA and GDPR. It is a difficult task to comprehend and abide by these rules when putting PPML into practice. More legislative changes are probably in the works, which will affect how businesses handle machine learning and data protection.

- **Technological limitations**: Research on enhancing the efficacy and efficiency of privacy-preserving algorithms is still underway. To overcome these constraints, developments in fields like secure multi-party computation, federated learning, and homomorphic encryption will be essential.

Future Directions

- **Ethical considerations**: PPML's ethical ramifications are becoming more well-known. Ethical frameworks for PPML implementation might be one of the next paths, guaranteeing that algorithms adhere to both ethical and legal norms.

- **Collaboration and education**: It is essential to encourage cooperation between business, academics, and legislators. Organizations can negotiate the challenging landscape of data privacy laws and PPML implementation with the aid of knowledge exchange and instructional programs.

- **Democratization of PPML**: The democratization of PPML tools and processes will likely be a future trend. Making these technologies more accessible to a larger variety of enterprises, including smaller firms, can lead to widespread adoption.

6.6 Legal and Ethical Considerations in AI Security

1. **Data Privacy and Protection**

   - **Legal Considerations:** Regulations that govern the collection, storing, and processing of personal data include the CCPA in California, the GDPR in Europe, and other national or regional legislation. As Cloud security solutions incorporating ML/DL, threat mitigation should go hand-in-hand with maintaining privacy or users/customer data.

   - **Ethical Considerations:** To this end, while applying AI to threat detection it is crucial to avoid misusing personal data or exposing it. The individual privacy risks should be dealt with either by anonymization or pseudonymization techniques

2. **Bias and Fairness**

   - **Legal Considerations:** It is prohibited to bring about unfair discrimination by the operation of an AI system. Historical prejudice of programmers can prompt algorithms to smear some people based on gender, race or economic status. This is especially relevant with respect to anti-discrimination standards which most organizations have to adhere to within nations. Systems that original in a biased form could be in direct contravention of obligations relating to equal treatment as per the law.

3. **Ethical Considerations:** Therefore, there is the need to apply fairness, accountability and openness in the ML models transparency and accountability in the ML models used in threat detection. To make it safe to use the model should not learn or reinforce some bias that is unhealthy for society or has negative influences. Such risks

may be managed by the use of techniques such as fairness constraints and constant model auditing.

4. **Accountability and Transparency**

- **Legal Considerations:** AI-driven Cloud database security solutions should be able to identify specific actors either within the system or at the organizational level who are held responsible for the duties performed by the system. In case an AI-based system is unable to identify a security threat in its environment, it is important to ascertain the entity at fault (be it, Cloud service provider, developers or users). Transparency is also critical when interacting with essential infrastructure or moreover, influential data.

- **Ethical Considerations:** The last ethical requirement is that of aspiring to create transparency as to the decision-making processes concerning the functioning of algorithms for purposes such as threat detection alert so that different stakeholders can comprehend the cognitive approaches to decision-making by the artificial intelligence underpinning the actions being taken. This is the reason why a lack of explain ability could cause a distrust of the system.

5. **Data Sovereignty and Jurisdiction**

- **Legal Considerations:** For AI used in Cloud database security, data sovereignty laws should be considered as laws that describe where data may be stored and how it may be stored particularly if it is to be stored in a number of regions or countries. Some of the main legal risks relate to overseas data movement, particularly to laws such as GDPR.

- **Ethical Considerations:** Data ethical handling should include making sure that any sensitive data doesn't fall into the wrong hands in jurisdictions that do not respect the privacy of the individuals. The location of collection, storage and processing should be clearly communicated to the users of the organization.

6. Security of the AI System Itself

- **Legal Considerations:** Real-world AI systems employed in threat detection are susceptible to cyber threat or adversarial incline (e.g., in case of ML models). Cyber security laws including Cybersecurity Information Sharing Act (CISA) in the US mandates that organizations should protect their systems properly. AI systems should be designed such they cannot be manipulated or have vulnerabilities inserted in to them by an attacker.

- **Ethical Considerations:** Non-misuse respectful-use AI ethics include preventing the AI systems from being vulnerable to adversarial tampering and also the developers of the system trying to improve the defense against such attacks. It also means that application of ethical responsibility covers testing the system under as many realistic conditions as possible.

7. Informed Consent and User Awareness

- **Legal Considerations:** Some jurisdictions mean that users might have to opt-in as to how the data is used, particularly if the AI systems acting on the information are processing a user's personal or identifiable data. Any use of AI systems must be fully disclosed to Cloud providers and users must provide their consent.

- **Ethical Considerations:** People should be educative on the pros and cons of using Artificial Intelligent in security. This includes being able to know what happens to the personal data that they share when the companies train the machine learning models and when they detect threats and the implications of when the system is erroneous, or when it produces a false alarm.

8. Human Oversight

- **Legal Considerations:** Most jurisdictions expect that decisions made by an AI system to have some human intervention especially when the decision affects the legal or financial status of a person; the critical decision could be regarding security or user access approval. There should be ways by which humans can interject themselves into the decision-making processes of the artificial intelligence systems.

- **Ethical Considerations:** Ethical AI use aims at HITL systems under which human beings can analyze, dispute, or reject AI-made decisions. This way, the system isn't making fully automated decisions as it is resembled by a real moral agent.

9. **Incident Response and Liability**

- **Legal Considerations:** When there is a security breach, it is necessary to establish who has taken the wrong decision whether caused by AI or a person. Policies laid down by law should provide for accountability in the event where the threat is not detected by the AI system, or in the event that a breach was as a result of the AI system's output.

- **Ethical Considerations:** From an ethical perspective, there must always be laid down process on how each failure is handled and the organization's systems enhanced. This includes admitting to failure and informing the stakeholders about what happened and what the company intends on doing to fix it.

10. **Continuous Learning and Adaptability**

- **Legal Considerations:** That is, as the systems learn they might develop in ways that are not expected from their designers. This brings the question of how these emergent systems meet expectation of the existing laws and regulations.

- **Ethical Considerations:** That means ethical problems emerge when an AI system continues to develop and take actions or make choices that are unethical, for instance, raising the likelihood of false positives or being prejudiced against a particular workforce. The models used have to be monitored, audited, and updated frequently to prevent it from being used with unethical criteria.

6.7 Cloud Database Security Regulations and Compliance

Cloud compliance refers to following a set of rules and guidelines that are required for Cloud computing services. These guidelines, which are frequently established by governmental organizations, business associations, or internal guidelines, guarantee that data handled and kept in the Cloud is secure and utilized sensibly. Cloud compliance protects private data, protects sensitive information, and keeps Cloud service providers and their customers trusting each other. Given the increase in data breaches, compliance is essential for both operational security and consumer trust.

Components of Cloud Compliance

Making ensuring that Cloud usage complies with different legal, regulatory, and corporate norms requires a complex strategy known as Cloud compliance. Understanding and putting into practice the essential elements that regulate data management and security in the Cloud environment are necessary to achieve Cloud compliance. Any company using the Cloud must have these elements in order to comply with regulations and preserve data integrity.

- **Standards**

    A variety of best practices and benchmarks that specify how Cloud services should be utilized and maintained are included in standards for Cloud compliance. These include information security management frameworks such as ISO/IEC 27001, which offer a methodical way to handle confidential enterprise data. Following these guidelines guarantees the security of Cloud infrastructure and the effectiveness of Cloud operations for companies. Adherence to these guidelines improves security and increases client confidence in Cloud service providers. To satisfy Cloud compliance requirements, Cloud service providers must make sure their offerings are in line with these standards.

- **Laws and regulations**

  Laws and regulations dictate legal requirements for companies that use Cloud services, making them an essential component of Cloud compliance. One well-known example is the General Data Protection Regulation (GDPR), which enforces stringent guidelines for individual data protection and privacy inside the European Union. To avoid fines and keep customers' trust, businesses must comprehend and abide by these requirements. This involves making certain that their Cloud provider conforms with applicable rules, particularly when managing private or sensitive data. Because rules are always changing, navigating these laws is a constant task.

- **Governance**

  The policies and processes that companies set up to manage their Cloud usage are referred to as governance in Cloud compliance. Cloud services are employed in a way that satisfies company goals and regulatory requirements thanks to effective governance. This entails establishing precise guidelines for risk management, access control, and data security in the Cloud environment. Robust governance frameworks help Cloud service providers achieve Cloud compliance standards on a regular basis. Additionally, it entails routinely reviewing and modifying these rules to conform to changing business requirements and compliance environments.

- **Audits**

  An essential part of Cloud compliance is audits, which give companies a way to confirm that their Cloud services and infrastructure adhere to relevant laws and standards. These audits frequently entail a careful analysis of the Cloud provider's data processing, storage, and security procedures. Frequent audits assist companies in finding areas for Cloud use enhancement and compliance gaps. They are also an essential instrument for proving compliance to stakeholders and authorities. Maintaining continuous Cloud compliance requires selecting a Cloud provider that supports and allows frequent compliance audits.

Important of Cloud compliance

Cloud compliance is essential for any Cloud-based organisation. It guarantees that Cloud services adhere to ethical and legal norms and are utilized responsibly. For companies, maintaining Cloud compliance means protecting their operations, brand, and clientele. It goes beyond simply adhering to regulations.

- **Data protection and privacy:** Protecting sensitive data from breaches and unwanted access requires effective Cloud compliance procedures. Businesses may lower the risk of data leaks and the related legal and reputational consequences by following compliance rules, which guarantee that sensitive and personal information is handled securely.

- **Legal and regulatory adherence:** Businesses that operate in the Cloud must abide by rules and regulations like the GDPR. Legal penalties and fines, which may be severe and detrimental to a company's financial stability and reputation, are avoided by this commitment.

- **Business continuity and risk management:** Planning for business continuity and risk management both heavily rely on Cloud compliance. It assists in recognizing and reducing the risks connected to Cloud use, making sure that compliance issues or data security breaches don't interfere with corporate operations.

- **Customer trust and loyalty:** Consumers are calling for greater data security and transparency. Following Cloud compliance guidelines gives clients peace of mind that their data is being handled appropriately, which promotes loyalty and confidence.

- **Competitive advantage:** In a market where a lot of companies use Cloud services, compliance may set you apart. Strong compliance procedures may provide businesses a competitive edge by drawing in clients and partners that respect ethical behaviour and data protection.

Best Practices for Cloud Compliance

Adopting best practices is essential for companies using Cloud services to guarantee that they satisfy regulatory standards and safeguard sensitive data. Achieving Cloud compliance is a continuous process that calls for a strategic approach to data management and security in the Cloud.

1. **Understand the shared responsibility model:** Compliance in Cloud computing is a joint duty between the customer and the Cloud provider. In general, the client is in charge of protecting the data they store in the Cloud, even while the Cloud provider guarantees the security of the Cloud infrastructure. Businesses must completely comprehend their role in upholding compliance under this shared responsibility approach, especially in areas like data encryption and access control. Potential weaknesses in security and compliance procedures can be found with the aid of a thorough grasp of this common model.

2. **Assess your compliance requirements:** Every company has to carefully evaluate its unique compliance needs in light of its activities and data. This entails being aware of the pertinent laws and rules, such as GDPR for businesses that handle the data of EU residents or HIPAA for data pertaining to healthcare in the United States. It is essential to update these evaluations on a regular basis since company operations and the regulatory environment might change, requiring adjustments to compliance strategy.

3. **Know the security risks specific to your business:** Effective Cloud compliance requires recognizing and resolving the particular security threats relevant to your industry. The Payment Card Industry Data Security Standard (PCI DSS), for instance, must be strictly adhered to by companies in the financial technology industry that handle credit card transactions. To secure cardholder data, this entails putting

strict data security measures in place, including as encryption, access restriction, and frequent security audits. Maintaining compliance and protecting sensitive financial data need an understanding of and attention to these sector-specific risks, such as possible weaknesses in transaction processing or data storage.

4. **Protect your data through encryption:** One essential procedure for protecting data in a Cloud setting is encryption. Businesses may drastically lower the risk of illegal access and data breaches that necessitate a security incident response by encrypting data both in transit and at rest. It is particularly important to use strong encryption techniques when working with private or sensitive data. Furthermore, it's critical to handle encryption keys safely, making sure that only authorized individuals can access them and that they are shielded from outside dangers.

5. **Understand your service level agreement (SLA):** The conditions of service, including performance criteria, uptime, and data management rules, are outlined in the service level agreement (SLA) that you have with your Cloud service provider. For businesses to be sure that their SLA complies with their Cloud compliance standards, they must carefully examine and comprehend it. This comprehension aids in establishing unambiguous expectations and duties, and it makes apparent the potential remedies and mitigation measures in the case of a service outage or data breach.

6. **Setup and monitor access control to your Cloud infrastructure:** To prevent breaches and illegal use of Cloud infrastructure, effective access control is crucial. To guarantee that only authorized personnel have access to critical information and applications, this entails putting in place strict user permissions and authentication procedures. Maintaining a secure Cloud environment requires regular monitoring and upgrading of access restrictions to keep up with changes in roles and persons. For further protection, companies should think about using multi-factor authentication.

7. **Conduct regular audits for risk assessment:** Identifying and reducing hazards in the Cloud environment requires regular assessments. Compliance with corporate rules, security procedures, and regulatory obligations should all be evaluated during these audits. Businesses may take prompt remedial action by identifying vulnerabilities and non-compliance concerns early on through these audits. Additionally, audits offer insightful information about the efficacy of the present Cloud compliance measures and areas for development(Digital ocean, 2023).

Cloud Security Compliance

The practice of following rules intended to safeguard information, guarantee privacy, and preserve security in Cloud computing environments is known as Cloud security compliance. These rules may be included into laws, created by governments, upheld by businesses, or specified in contracts. Organizations must have policies, controls, and processes in place to safeguard any data they keep, process, or send over the Cloud in order to comply.

Regulations and standards for data protection serve as the boundaries for Cloud security compliance. These are some essential standards to be aware of:

- **HIPAA:** Organisations must handle protected health information (PHI) in accordance with the Health Insurance Portability and Accountability Act (HIPAA). It is a national standard that was created in the US to safeguard American patients' private information.

- **PCI DSS:** Credit card information must be protected according to the Payment Card Industry Data Security Standard (PCI DSS). Keeping payment data safe at all times is crucial since its life cycle is far longer than the moment of a transaction.

- **GDPR:** Regardless of the nature, purpose, or location of processing, the General Data Protection Regulation (GDPR) is a privacy regulation created in the European Union to protect the data of its residents. One of the most stringent data security regulations in the world, GDPR seeks to safeguard private information as a human right.

Certifications and guidelines for Cloud security are additional crucial elements of compliance. These major organisations in the field give businesses best practices and established criteria for keeping Cloud systems safe:

- **CCM:** A thorough foundation for Cloud security is offered by the Cloud Controls Matrix (CCM), which was developed by the Cloud Security Alliance (CSA). The matrix is divided into 17 domains and 197 objectives that collectively address all of the important facets of Cloud computing and the most effective means of securing and safeguarding them.

- **NIST:** As another well-known collection of standards, the National Institute of Standards and Technology (NIST) Cybersecurity Framework offers recommendations for controlling and reducing cybersecurity threats. As the threat landscape and Cloud technology evolve, NIST regularly updates the framework.

- **ISO:** One of the most extensively used international standards for information security management systems, including Cloud-based systems, is ISO/IEC 27001, which is maintained by the International Organisation for Standardisation (ISO). An organization's cybersecurity compliance is promoted through a third-party ISO certification.

- **SOC2:** Organisations can also offer independent compliance verification through System and Organisation Controls (SOC) 2 certifications. A third-party audit of your compliance with accepted Cloud security guidelines might significantly improve your standing as a reliable company in the industry.

Challenges to Cloud Security Compliance

Because of the nature of Cloud technology, Cloud security compliance is often hampered by some of common issues. For businesses looking to protect hybrid and multi-cloud Cloud infrastructures, the first is relevant. Additional Cloud governance procedures are necessary to maintain compliance since these arrangements are by nature more complicated than single platforms. Clear rules and procedures for Cloud usage, including administrative controls, access management, and data protection measures, must be established by organizations using multi-cloud or hybrid Cloud systems.

Ensuring data privacy and Cloud security compliance across national boundaries is the second significant difficulty that organizations may encounter. Governments are the source of some of the laws and guidelines that need compliance, including GDPR. This indicates that various nations have unique privacy and data protection laws, and that these laws might range greatly in terms of their standards and methods of enforcement.

Everywhere they conduct business, organizations must manage the complex web of rules to guarantee compliance and safeguard sensitive data. For some businesses, that means striking a balance between the company's location and the users' locations. When it comes to Cloud security compliance, cross-border data transfers are a bigger problem for multinational corporations.

5 Strategies for Enhancing Cloud Security Compliance

1. **Identify and understand compliance requirements:** Start by going over and evaluating the particular rules and guidelines that are relevant to your sector and the areas where your company works. By doing this, your team will be better able to create a thorough plan

and put the controls in place needed to meet and stay in compliance with industry standards and legal requirements.

2. **Implement robust access control measures:** Organizations must set up uniform access management procedures in order to comply. Make regular use of robust authentication techniques to confirm the identity of your users. Access restrictions should also be put in place to guarantee that users may only access the resources they require at the appropriate time. Your security team may assign the right rights depending on the needs and behaviours of each individual user by using a zero-trust approach.

3. **Audit and assess your compliance regularly:** Being compliant is never a one-time event. Being in compliance and keeping it needs constant, committed work. To ensure Cloud security compliance, internal evaluations and compliance audits are crucial. In order to find flaws or vulnerabilities and make the necessary adjustments, organizations must routinely analyze and assess their security controls and procedures.

4. **Use encryption and data loss prevention tools:** Since encryption prevents unauthorized users from reading data, it is an essential step in safeguarding sensitive information both in transit and at rest. By monitoring and managing data flows, data loss prevention (DLP) systems assist stop breaches, leaks, and illegal access. DLP services and encryption collaborate to maintain data integrity from several perspectives. If an attacker manages to penetrate a system, the former guarantees that they cannot access any sensitive data, while the latter makes it more difficult for them to succeed. These tools work together to assist organizations in meeting data security laws and regulations. They also offer reporting features and audit trails, which are crucial for proving compliance with Cloud security.

5. **Automate compliance monitoring with CASB:** Additionally, your company may automate compliance monitoring with the use of technological instruments. For instance, a Cloud access security

broker (CASB) serves as a security checkpoint between Cloud service providers and users. Organizations may comply with data protection, access control, and threat prevention regulations and enforce policies with the assistance of CASBs. Security teams can accomplish, monitor, and maintain compliance more effectively if all these compliance-related tasks are combined into a single technological solution.(Lookout, 2024).

6.8 Integrating Hybrid AI and Cloud Security Solutions

What is hybrid Cloud security?

Software-defined networking (SDN), virtualization, and application support at every service mesh layer spanning several data centers and hardware components are all part of hybrid Cloud security. Businesses are increasingly looking for "single pane of glass" administration for hybrid Cloud networking, which combines enhanced real-time data packet analytics with all the functionality of conventional network administration and data centre management software. Hybrid Cloud security has to accommodate new, cutting-edge software platforms that haven't been fully validated in production and function at all dispersed network layers. Network administrators have particular challenges with hybrid Cloud security, which are best solved by tools and utilities incorporated into SDN orchestration channels through embedded SIEM programs that do real-time data packet scanning, monitoring, and network analytics.

Because hybrid Cloud computing supports the de facto methods of operation for thousands of employees or several software development teams working today, IT experts in large business organizations select it. Because of the way the present IT environment functions, company managers have to compare public Cloud providers based on support for proprietary or open-source software services and the price of commodity hardware. In the past 10 years, senior business management has quickly embraced Cloud outsourcing for the vast majority of software services that are visible to the public throughout the Fortune 500. Nonetheless, the majority of these high-ranking decision-makers continue to forbid the remote hosting of extremely sensitive files and data outside of an on-site data center. The main feature of hybrid Cloud architecture is its necessity to accommodate on-premises data centers or private Cloud hardware; nevertheless, security experts face particular problems and difficulties with this type of networking.

Hybrid Cloud security challenges

Securing hybrid Cloud environments and workflows can be challenging because hybrid Clouds are especially complex – and that complexity can give rise to unique security challenges that don't exist in other types of Cloud or on-prem architectures.

1. **Diverse infrastructure:** By definition, a hybrid Cloud includes multiple infrastructure components or platforms. This diversity creates security challenges because it's more difficult to enforce security best practices across disparate platforms than it is if all of your workloads reside in a single environment. In contrast to managing access rights in the public Cloud portion of your hybrid environment using the Identity and Access Management (IAM) framework of a public Cloud provider, your private data center could not support IAM. This leads to greater complexity – and more opportunity to introduce configuration mistakes that could lead to security risks – in the hybrid environment.

2. **Varying user identities:** The way you manage user identities may also vary between the public and private portions of a hybrid Cloud environment. For instance, you might use a public Cloud provider's authentication service when users log into public Cloud infrastructure but rely on a separate authentication provider to manage access to private infrastructure.

3. The complexity of user management within hybrid Cloud environments may lead to security risks because it makes it more challenging to avoid issues like giving users excessive permissions.

4. **Inconsistent visibility:** Your level of visibility into different parts of a hybrid Cloud environment may vary. In general, you'll have more visibility into and control over private infrastructure than over the public Cloud portion of your hybrid Cloud, since you own only the private infrastructure.

5. This means that you may not be able to monitor all parts of the Cloud environment in a consistent way, making it more challenging to discover security threats and risks.

6. **Inconsistent security tooling:** In some cases, security tools may only work with certain parts of your hybrid Cloud environment. This is especially likely if you use security monitoring services offered by public Cloud providers, whose solutions usually don't support private or on-prem infrastructure, even if said infrastructure forms part of a hybrid Cloud.

Understanding the Hybrid Cloud Security Architecture

The exact way that hybrid Cloud security solutions work can vary. But in general, the key architectural components of hybrid Cloud security include software services that operate at the convergence of the public and private parts of the hybrid Cloud environment. From there, the services deliver security capabilities such as:

- Enforcement of consistent access controls to manage who can do what across the hybrid Cloud.

- Features of Data Loss Prevention (DLP), which assist in identifying private information that could not be properly kept.

- Vulnerability scanning and management, to identify security risks within applications deployed in the hybrid Cloud.

- Data encryption lowers the possibility of unwanted access as it travels across the Cloud.

- Network segmentation, which can help reduce security risks by isolating workloads at the network level.

- Backup and disaster recovery, to help recover quickly in the event of a hybrid Cloud breach.

- Monitoring of network traffic, access logs, application requests, and other data sources to detect potential security risks.

By providing these security capabilities as services that work in a unified way across both the public and private parts of the hybrid Cloud environment, hybrid Cloud security solutions make it easier to secure hybrid environments without having to juggle disparate security tools and frameworks.

Key Components of Hybrid Cloud Security

Sources: - *(Jose Ignacio Fernandez del Campo Aguado, 2020)*

6.9 Chapter Summary

This chapter is devoted to the issue of multi-Cloud/hybrid Cloud security, which is a relevant topic because these models offer flexibility at the price of managing heterogeneous environments. They are phishing, malware, and ransomware, and in addressing them with network segmentation and encryption and intrusion detection. The chapter also discusses the effects of quantum computing on classical cryptography stating that it is vulnerable, and this calls for post-quantity technologies such QKD. Differential privacy and federated learning, two privacy-preserving ML, strategies are mentioned as a method of protecting the data. Moreover, it advances the research problem's legal and ethical elements in the area of AI security, focusing on regulations such as GDPR, AI fairness, and human supervision. The chapter recognizes a multidisciplinary approach towards Cloud and AI in order to address the issues of security, compliance, and risk management for data.

Multiple-choice questions (MCQs)

1. What is the growing complexity of cloud database environments primarily due to?

    a. The need for faster data storage

    b. The increasing number of cloud services and interconnections across multiple platforms

    c. The use of open-source databases only

    d. The limited number of cloud providers available

2. Which of the following is an emerging security threat in cloud database environments?

    a. Hardware failures

    b. Insider attacks and data breaches due to weak authentication mechanisms

    c. Server cooling issues

    d. Over-provisioning of cloud resources

3. **What role does quantum computing play in cloud database security?**

   a. It speeds up traditional encryption methods

   b. It may break current encryption schemes and require the development of quantum-resistant security algorithms

   c. It is irrelevant to cloud security

   d. It improves database storage capacity

4. **How do privacy-preserving machine learning techniques contribute to cloud database security?**

   a. By encrypting data before analysis

   b. By allowing machine learning models to be trained on encrypted data without exposing sensitive information

   c. By reducing the need for cloud infrastructure

   d. By simplifying data transfer between cloud platforms

5. **What is a significant legal and ethical consideration in AI security for cloud databases?**

   a. Whether AI systems can autonomously update security protocols

   b. The balance between security measures and user privacy, including compliance with data protection laws

   c. The use of AI to automate all decision-making processes

   d. Whether cloud service providers should offer free security features

6. **Which of the following is a challenge in maintaining cloud database security regulations and compliance?**

   a. Ensuring the scalability of cloud databases

   b. Adapting to changing regulatory requirements across different regions and jurisdictions

   c. Preventing hardware failures in cloud servers

   d. Reducing storage costs for cloud data

7. **How can integrating hybrid AI and cloud security solutions help enhance cloud database security?**

    a. By replacing cloud security providers with AI

    b. By combining the strengths of AI for threat detection with the flexibility and scalability of cloud solutions

    c. By allowing cloud providers to reduce security investments

    d. By automating data storage processes

8. **What is one of the main concerns with the increasing complexity of cloud database environments?**

    a. Reduced data processing speed

    b. Increased difficulty in monitoring and securing interconnected services and systems

    c. Limited scalability

    d. Lack of available cloud storage space

9. **Why is quantum computing a potential threat to cloud database security?**

    a. It speeds up encryption processes

    b. It can break traditional encryption methods, potentially compromising cloud data security

    c. It enables better data backup strategies

    d. It eliminates the need for cloud security protocols

10. **What is the primary challenge associated with privacy-preserving machine learning in cloud security?**

    a. Lack of availability of cloud computing resources

    b. Ensuring that privacy is maintained without sacrificing model accuracy and performance

    c. Reducing the complexity of machine learning models

    d. The high cost of implementing encryption techniques

Answers

1	2	3	4	5	6	7	8	9	10
B	B	B	B	B	B	B	B	B	B

BIBLIOGRAPHY

Hacks, C. (2024). Federated Learning: A Paradigm Shift in Data Privacy and Model Training. In *Medium*.

Akitra. (2024). *Managing Compliance in Multi-Cloud Environments: Leveraging Compliance as Code.*

Aliyev, S. (2017). *What is Blockchain Security in Cloud Computing_ - Swiss Cyber Institute.*

Aquasec. (2024). *Top 7 Cloud Security Challenges and How to Overcome Them.* Aquasec.

Bhuyan, A. P. (2017). *Understanding Homomorphic Encryption_ Enabling Secure Data Processing and Addressing Practical Challenges.*

Cameron F. Kerry. (2020). *Protecting privacy in an AI-driven world.* BROOKINGS.

Chain. (2024). *How to Strengthen Your Cloud Security with Blockchain Technology _ by Chain _ Medium.*

Chen, M., & Cui, S. (2024). *Federated Learning for Mobile Edge Computing* (pp. 151–170). https://doi.org/10.1007/978-3-031-51266-7_7

Cloud, G. (2023). *What is cloud data security? Benefits and solutions.* GOOGLLE CLOUD.

CloudMatos. (2024). *The Role of Threat Intelligence in Cloud Security*. Linkedin.

Daffodil. (2023). *The Role of AI-driven Patch Management in Cybersecurity*. https://insights.daffodilsw.com/blog/ai-driven-patch-management-in-cybersecurity

Digital ocean. (2023). *Understanding Cloud Compliance For Data Security and Privacy*. Digital Ocean.

Dulari. (2022). *Privacy-Preserving in Machine Learning (PPML)*. Analytics Vidhya.

Geeksforgeeks. (2024). *Feature Selection Techniques in Machine Learning*. Geeksforgeeks.Org.

geeksforgreeks. (2024). Emerging Attack Vectors in Cyber Security. *Geeksforgreeks*.

Greeksforgreeks. (2024). *Types of Databases*. Greeksforgreeks.

Hacks, C. (2024). *Federated Learning: A Paradigm Shift in Data Privacy and Model Training*. https://medium.com/@cloudhacks_/federated-learning-a-paradigm-shift-in-data-privacy-and-model-training-a41519c5fd7e

IBM. (2024). *What is data exfiltration?* IBM.

J, S., Kanagasabapathi, K., Mahajan, K., Ahamad, S., Soumya, E., & Barthwal, S. (2023). AI-Enhanced Multi-Cloud Security Management: Ensuring Robust Cybersecurity in Hybrid Cloud Environments. *2023 International Conference on Innovative Computing, Intelligent Communication and Smart Electrical Systems (ICSES)*, 1–6. https://doi.org/10.1109/ICSES60034.2023.10465550

javatpoint. (2023). *Cloud Computing Tutorial.* Javatpoint.

Jose Ignacio Fernandez del Campo Aguado. (2020). *What is Hybrid Cloud Security?* Aqua.

Kuriakose, A. A. (2024). *Algomox Blog _ Enhancing Multi-Cloud Security with AI Integration.*

Lee, K. (2024). *The Relationship Between Edge Computing and Cloud Computing.*

Lookout. (2024). *Cloud Security Compliance: Ensuring Data Safety in the Cloud.* Lookout.

Malaviarachchi, U. T. (2024). *(9) Federated Learning_ Empowering Decentralized Data Processing _ LinkedIn.*

Muhammad Eissa. (2024). *The Crucial Role of Threat Intelligence in Modern SOC and Threat Prevention.* Linkedin.

Nagmetulla, A. (2020). The impact of blockchain on accounting. In *International Journal of Information and ....*

Nedunoori, V. (2024). *AI-Driven Security_ A Comprehensive Approach to Multi-Cloud Protection - AI Time Journal - Artificial Intelligence, Automation, Work and Business.*

Paseband, S., & Verisk. (2021). The Impact of Blockchain on Emerging Economies. *Journal of Applied Business and Economics, 23*(1). https://doi.org/10.33423/jabe.v23i1.4069

Qualizeal. (2024). *The Future of Security Testing: Leveraging Machine Learning for Injection Attack Detection and Prevention.* Qualizeal.

Rakibul Hasan Chowdhury, Nayem Uddin Prince, Salman Mohammad Abdullah, & Labonno Akter Mim. (2024). The role of predictive analytics in cybersecurity: Detecting and preventing threats. *World Journal of Advanced Research and Reviews*, 23(2), 1615–1623. https://doi.org/10.30574/wjarr.2024.23.2.2494

Relan, K. (2023). *Cloud Computing And Database Management System*. Esds.

SentinelOne. (2024a). *AI Threat Detection_ Leverage AI to Detect Security Threats*.

SentinelOne. (2024b). *Multi-Cloud Security Solutions_ Best 10 Tools in 2025*.

shashank. (2024). *The Role of Quantum Computing in the Future of Cloud Services- Cloud Computing Certification*. COMMUNITY.

Shokri, R., Stronati, M., Song, C., & Shmatikov, V. (2017). Membership Inference Attacks Against Machine Learning Models. *2017 IEEE Symposium on Security and Privacy (SP)*, 3–18. https://doi.org/10.1109/SP.2017.41

Squadcast. (2024). *Cloud Complexity: Orchestrating Resources in Multi-Cloud Environments*. Meadium.

SWEENEY, L. (2002). k-ANONYMITY: A MODEL FOR PROTECTING PRIVACY. *International Journal of Uncertainty, Fuzziness and Knowledge-Based Systems*, 10(05), 557–570. https://doi.org/10.1142/S0218488502001648

Tierpoint. (2024). *How to Overcome Cloud Complexity Challenges & Simplify Cloud*. Tierpoint.

Trackier. (2024). *Programmatic Media Buying.* https://trackier. com/glossary/programmatic-media-buying/

Tramèr, F., Zhang, F., Juels, A., Reiter, M. K., & Ristenpart, T. (2016). Stealing machine learning models via prediction APIs. *Proceedings of the 25th USENIX Security Symposium.*

University, V. (2024). *Potential Risks of Using Cloud Databases and Storage.*

Zscaler. (2024). *What Are Insider Threats_ _ Define, Types, and Mitigation.*

ABOUT THE AUTHORS

Rajendra Prasad Sola has over 20 years of experience in the IT industry and currently serves as a Technology Manager, specializing in Cloud, Database Architecture and Administration. Raj has also held a Multinational Manager role, overseeing teams in both the USA and India. Raj possesses niche expertise in areas such as Clustering & Engineered System Management, Performance Engineering, Automation Maturity Assessment, Disaster Recovery as well as System Administration. Raj has extensive exposure to multi-database technologies, including Teradata and MongoDB. A certified Cloud Architect, Raj has worked with diverse range of clients across various domains, including Banking, Telecom, Life Sciences and Retail, and has a strong understanding of ITIL processes. Raj lives in the Greater Bengaluru area, India, with his wife, Aruna, and their son, Dushyanth.

Nihar Malali is a technology veteran having worked for more than two decades in the field of technology management and leadership. Nihar currently holds the positions of Senior Director & Senior Solutions Architect at National Life Group and has extensive experience in Cloud Computing, Artificial Intelligence, and Data-Driven Technologies to develop secure and efficient solutions that help organizations to scale up and improve customers' satisfaction.

Nihar has strong technical background in fields like Data engineering, Machine learning, Micro-services, Enterprise integration and has worked extensively in designing and implementing systems on platforms like Azure, AWS & GCP. His coding practice includes languages such as Python, Java, Rust, and Angular JS together with leadership skills in team mentoring and setting up governance structures.

An accomplished author, Nihar has penned influential works, including Data Strategy in the Age of AI: Creating the Base for Long

Term Success and going Digital in the Age of AI: Contact Center and Back Office Evolution. A TOGAF certified architect with PSM-1, PMP, ALMI, and ASDA certifications, he still helps organizations perform in today's fast-growing digital environment. Nihar resides in Mumbai with his family and continues to have zeal for development and creativity using technology.

Praveen Madugula is a seasoned technology leader specializing in digital transformation within the insurance life and annuities domain.

With extensive experience in full-stack development, data analytics, and cloud platforms (Azure, AWS), he drives innovative solutions that enhance operational efficiency and customer experiences.

His expertise includes enterprise solutions delivery, system integration, architecture design, and leadership in managing global teams.

Currently, as a Principal Consultant at Techno Tasks Inc., he leads technology teams to deliver solutions for complex Risk and Finance projects, including actuarial modeling, financial reporting, general ledger and reinsurance.

Previously, at DXC Technology, Praveen played pivotal roles in agile development, web-based application delivery, and client customization for platforms like wmA and Assure.

His technical acumen spans languages like C#, Python, and Java, and tools such as Azure DevOps, SQL Server, and MongoDB. He holds a Bachelor of Technology in Electronics and Communication from JNTU University, India.

Praveen is passionate about driving digital transformation and delivering impactful technological advancements in the insurance sector.